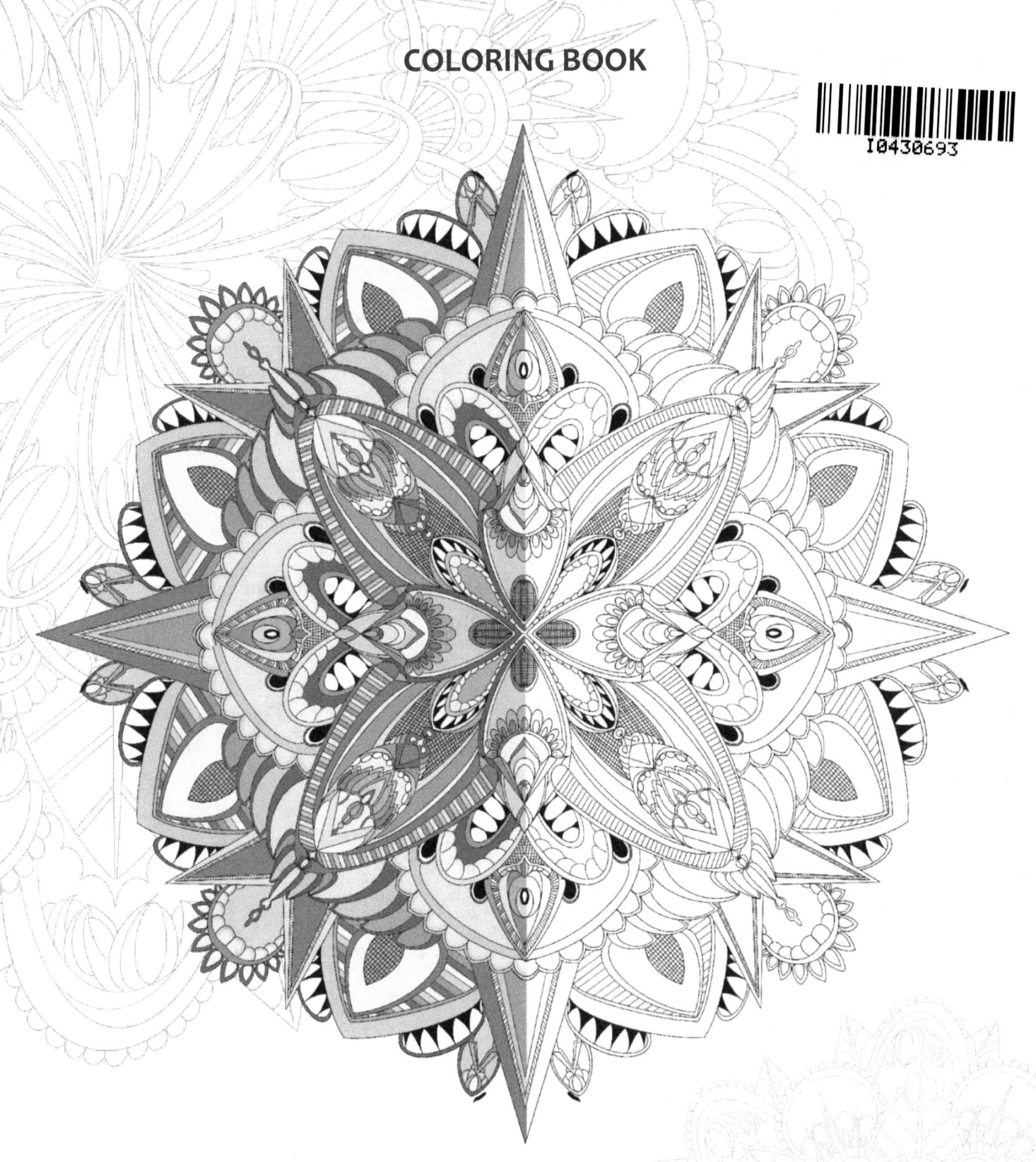

COLORING BOOK

MANDALAS
For Every Mood

Illustrations by Heidi Larson

Copyright © 2022, Heidi Larson. All rights reserved.

No part of this publication may be reproduced, stored in a retrieval system, or transmitted in any form or by any means, electronic, mechanical, photocopying, recording, or otherwise, without prior written permission of the author.

Permissions may be sought directly from Heidi Larson's Rights Department in Colorado, USA. You may complete your request online via the homepage:
 (https://www.hlcreativeservices.com),
by selecting "Contact", and completing the contact form.

Library of Congress Cataloging-in-Publication Data
Application Submitted.

ISBN: 9-798363836183

Illustrations by Heidi Larson

For information on all HL Creative works, visit our website at: www.hlcreativeservices.com
Printed in the United States of America

First Edition: December 2022
10 9 8 7 6 5 4 3 2 1

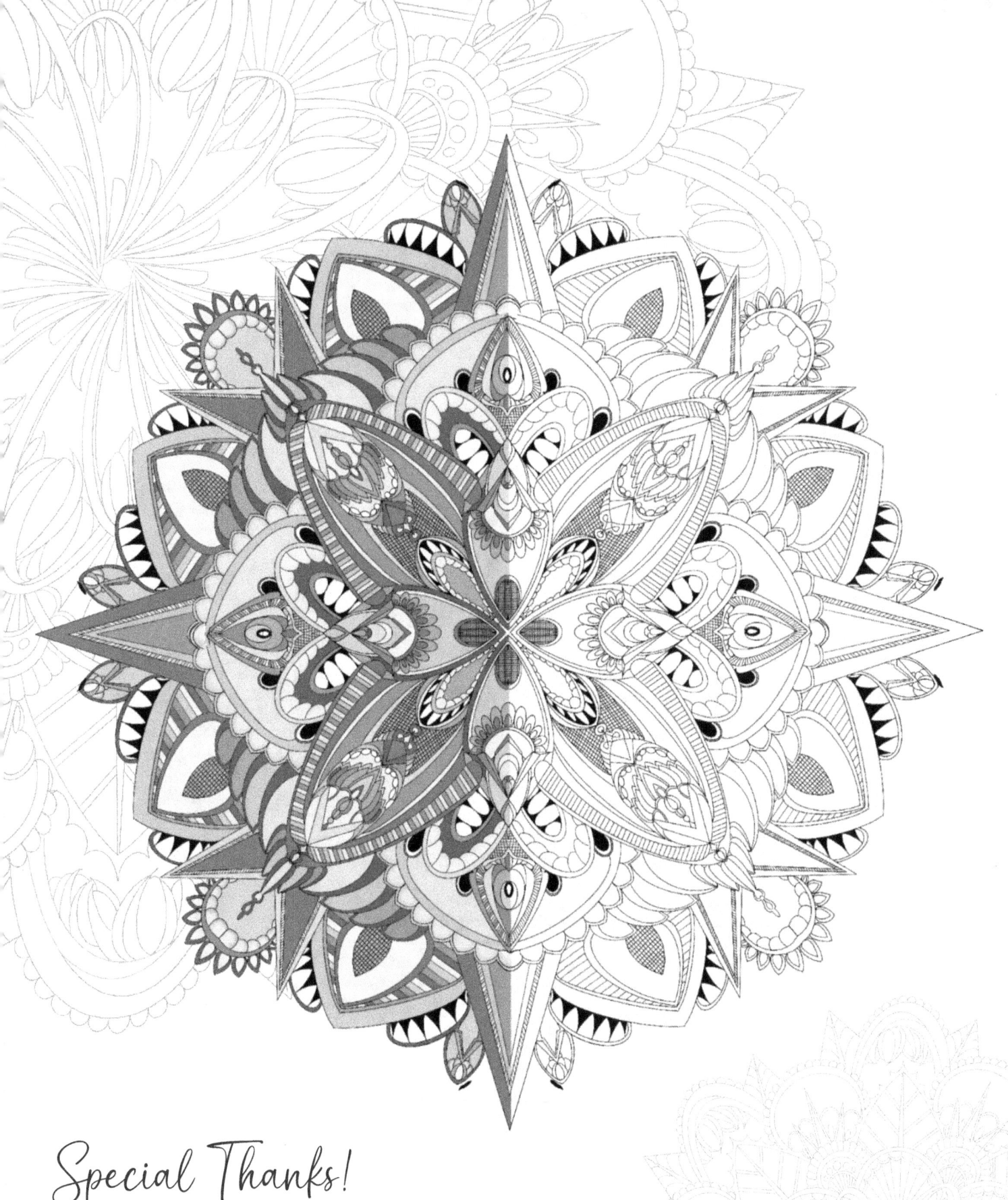

Special Thanks!

My greatest love and gratitude goes out to my family, friends, and my partner Michael for their love and support; and my sister, Gretchen for also pushing me to finally finish this thing!

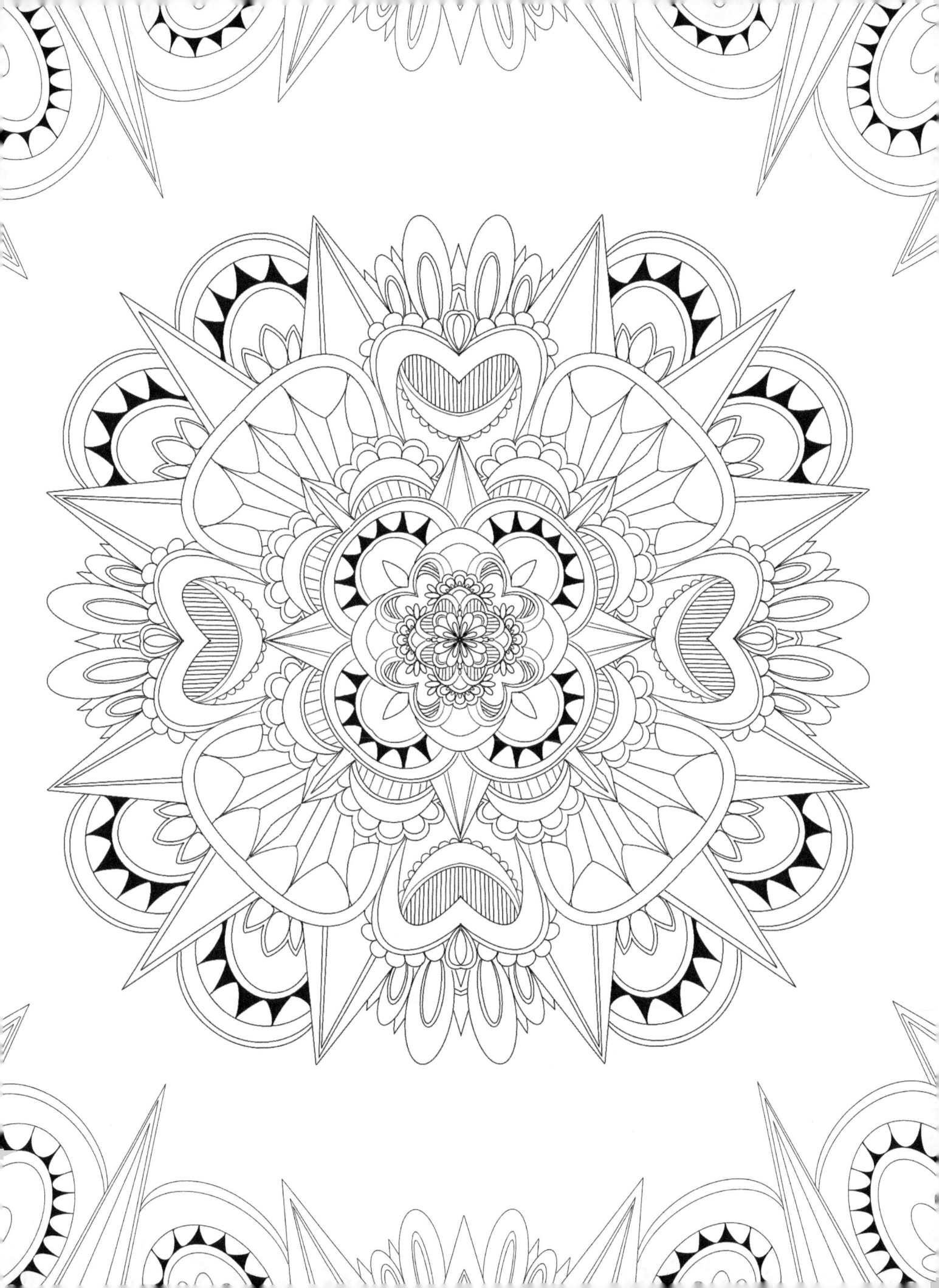

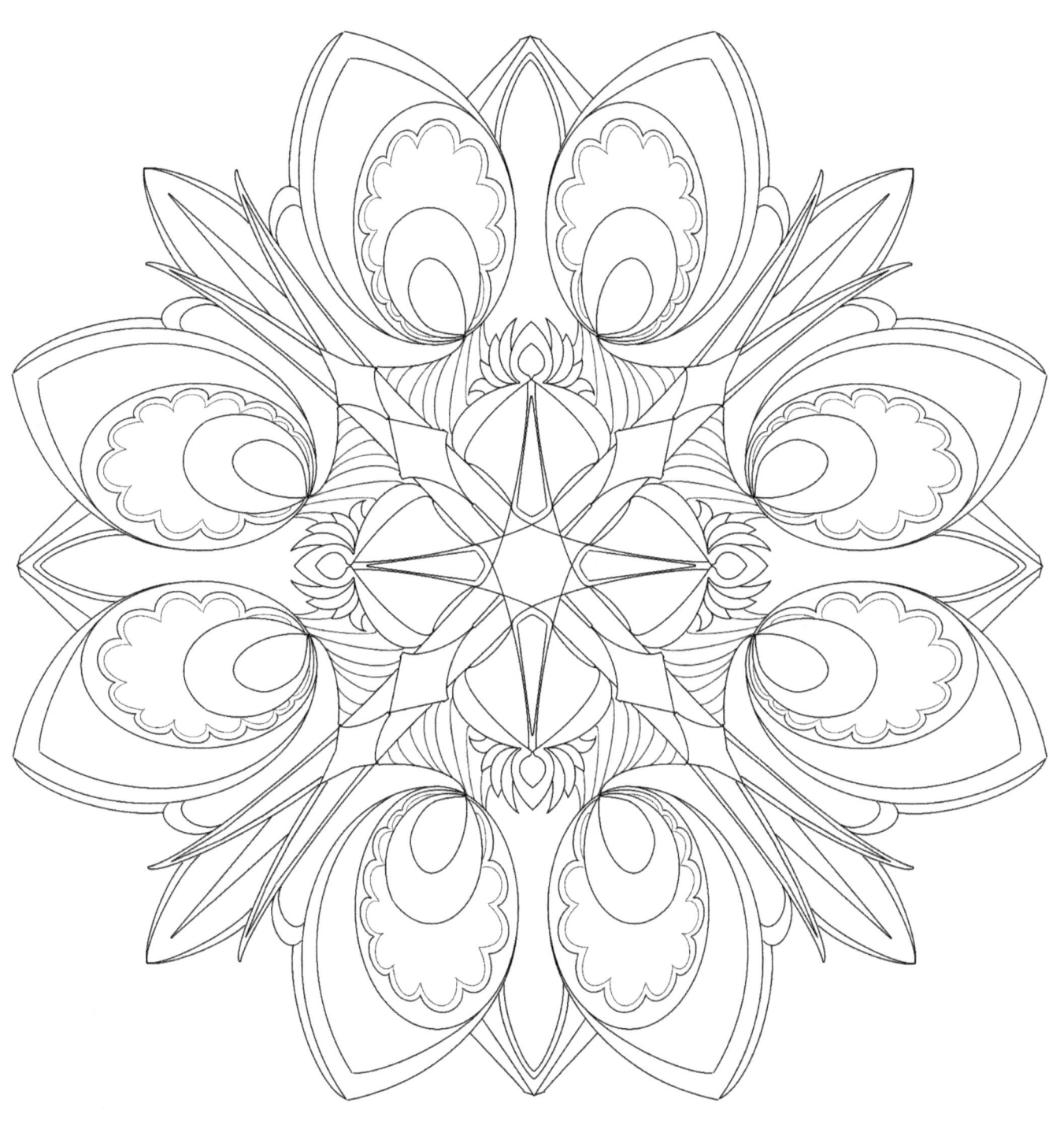

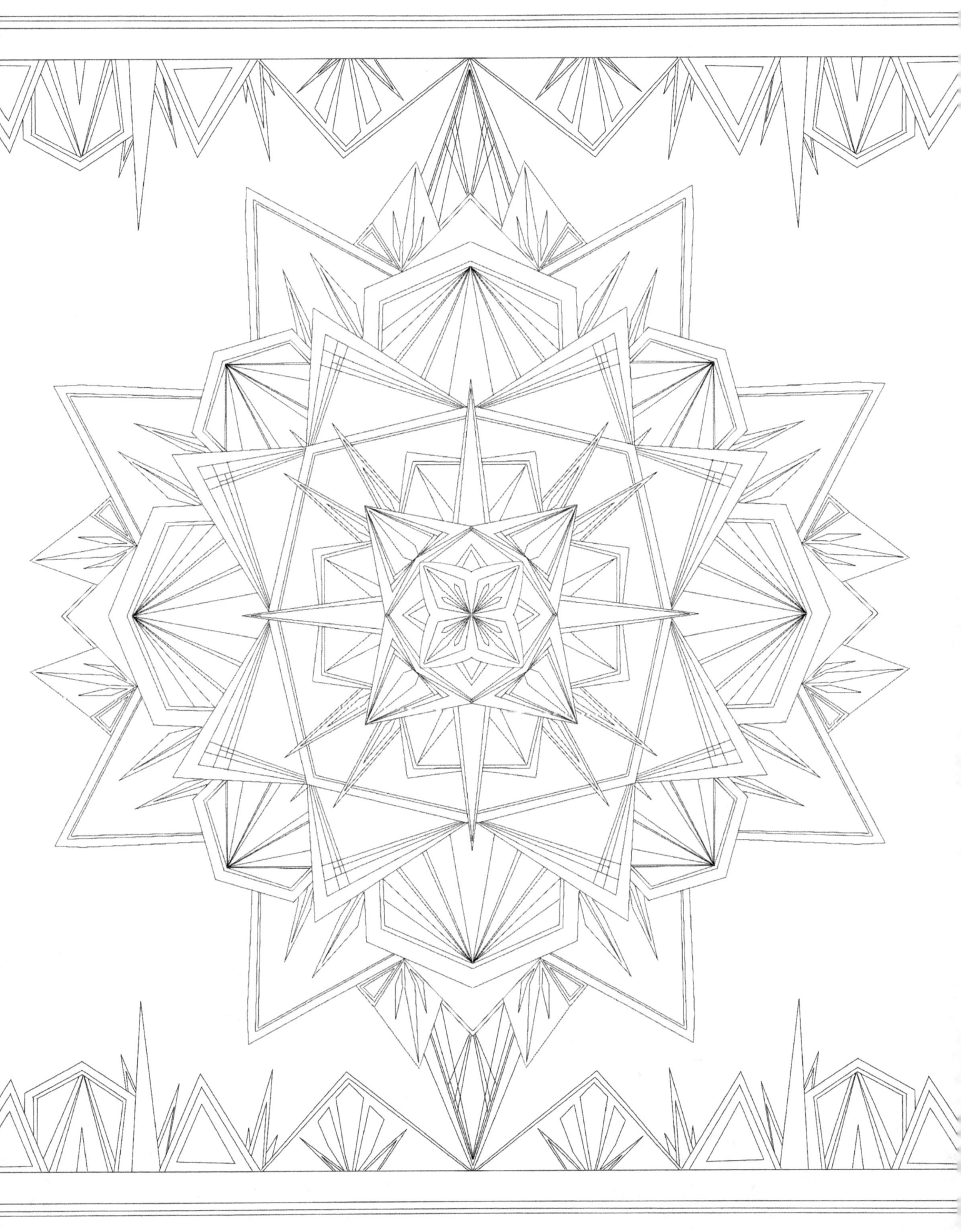

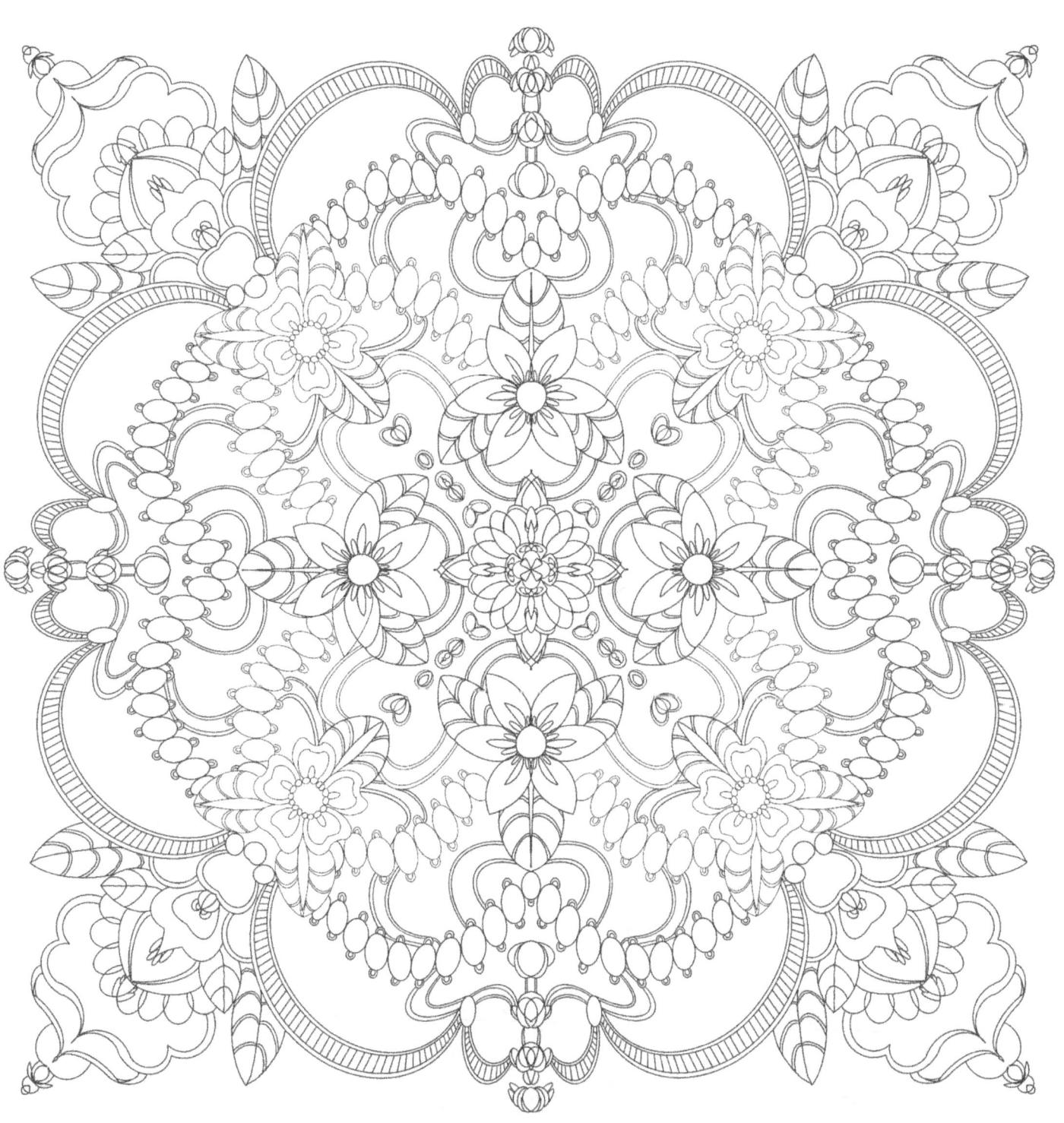

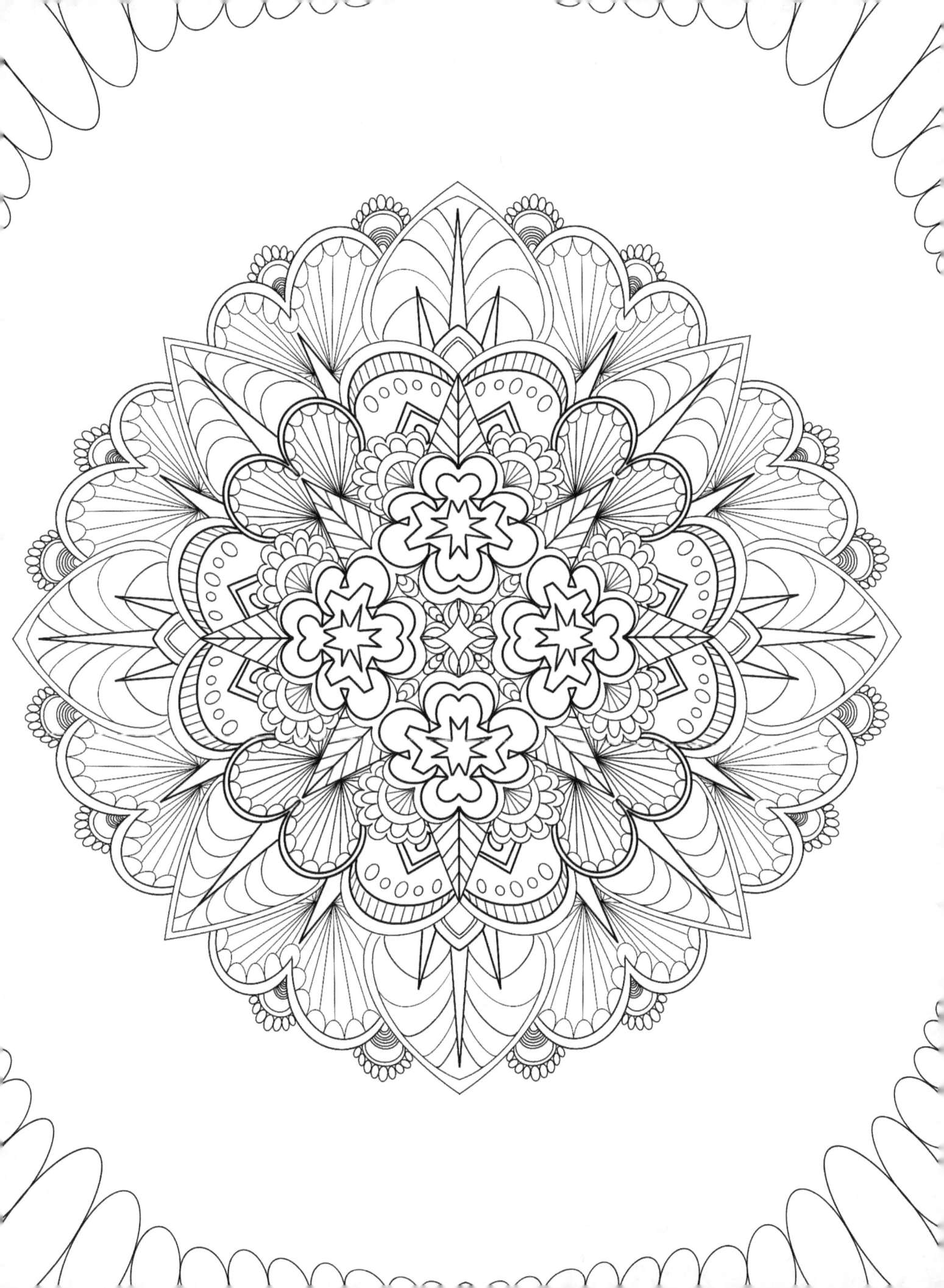

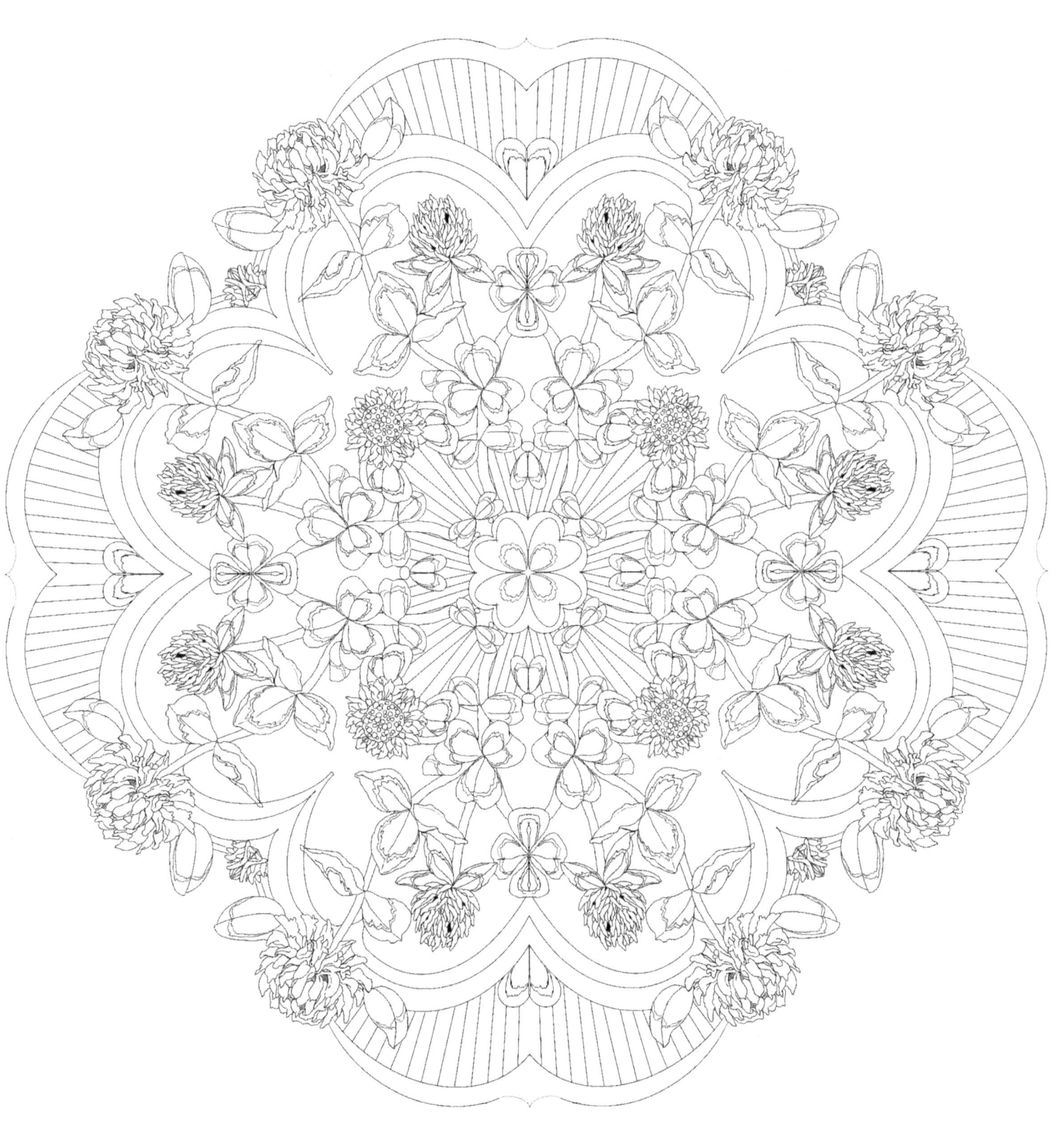

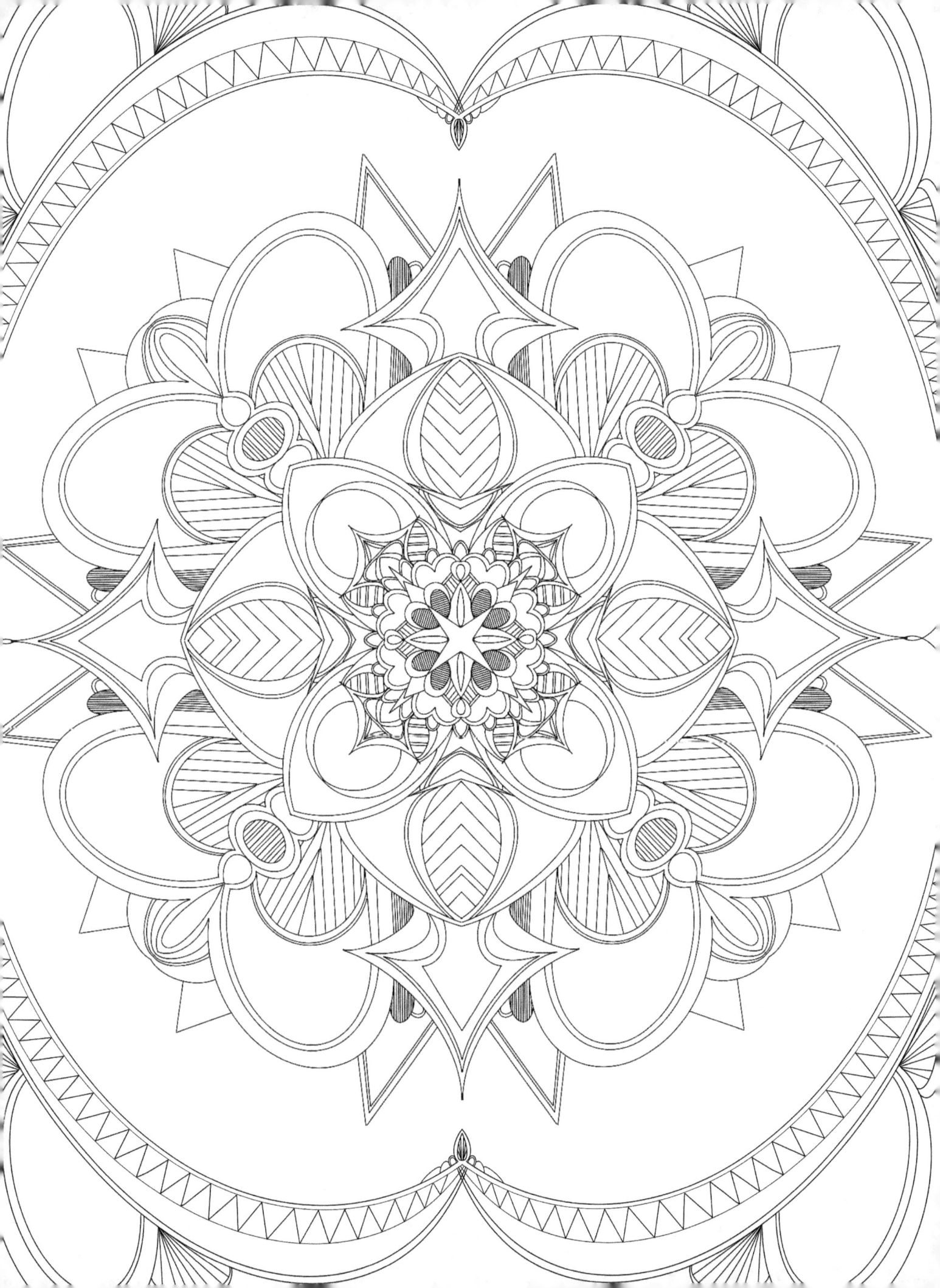

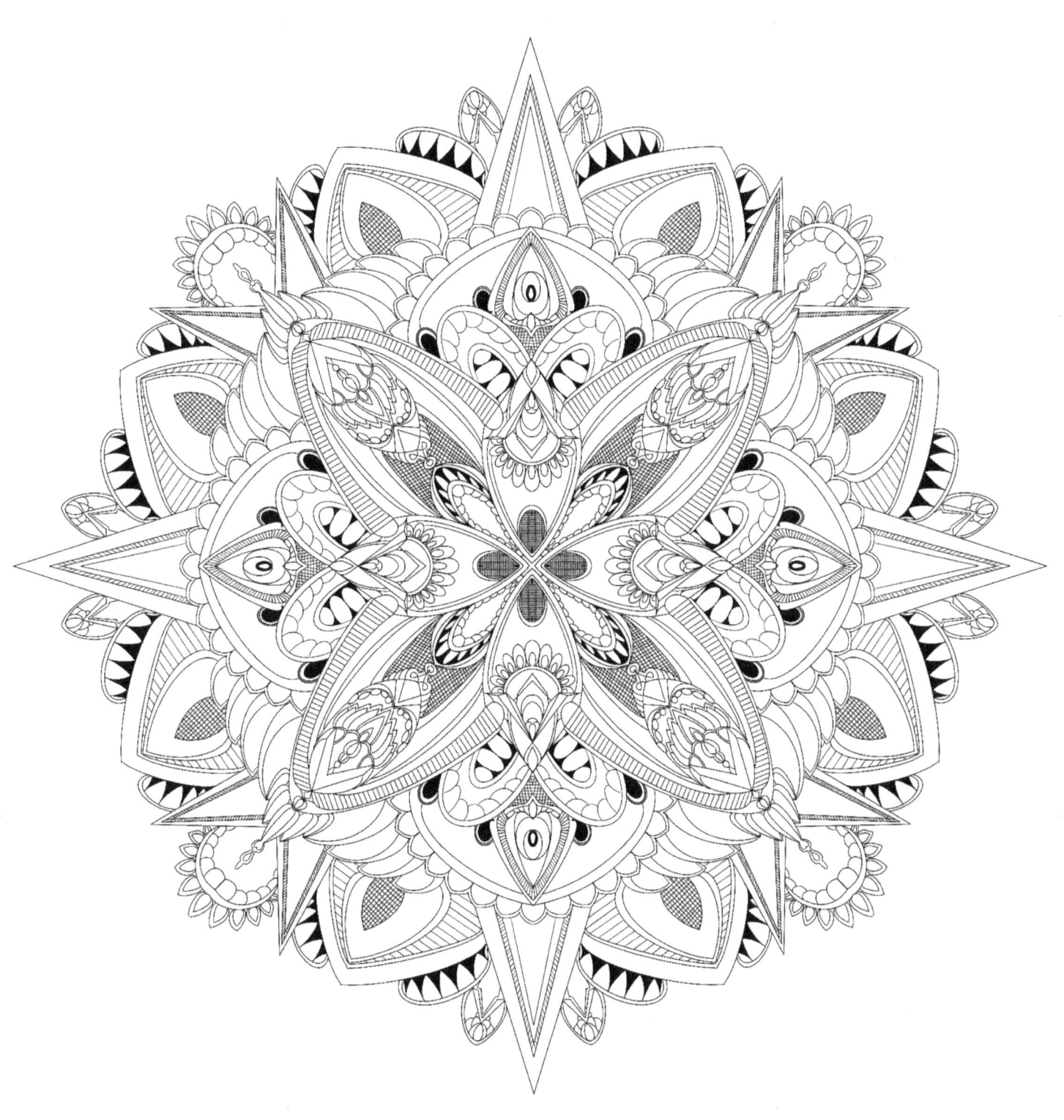

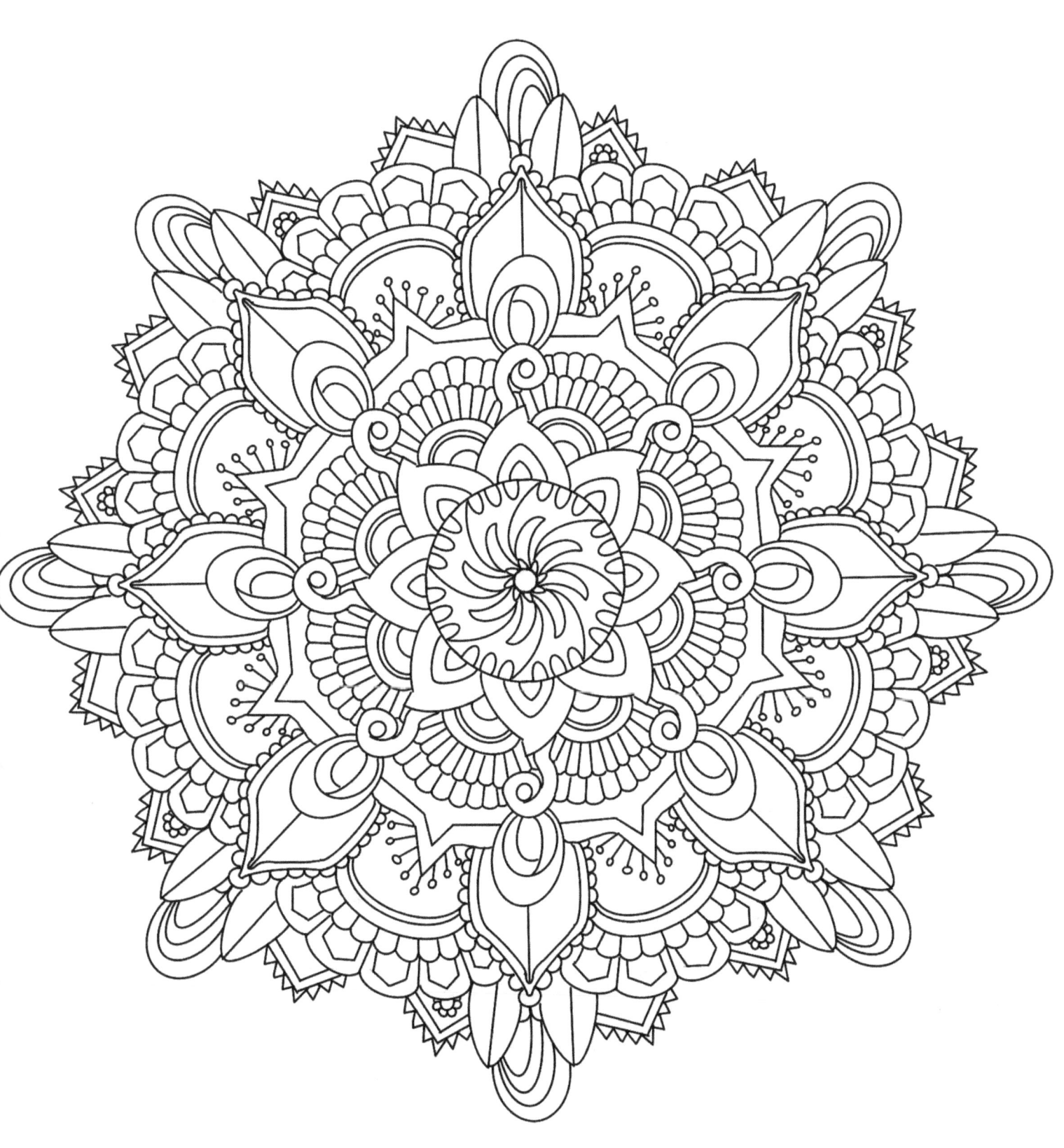

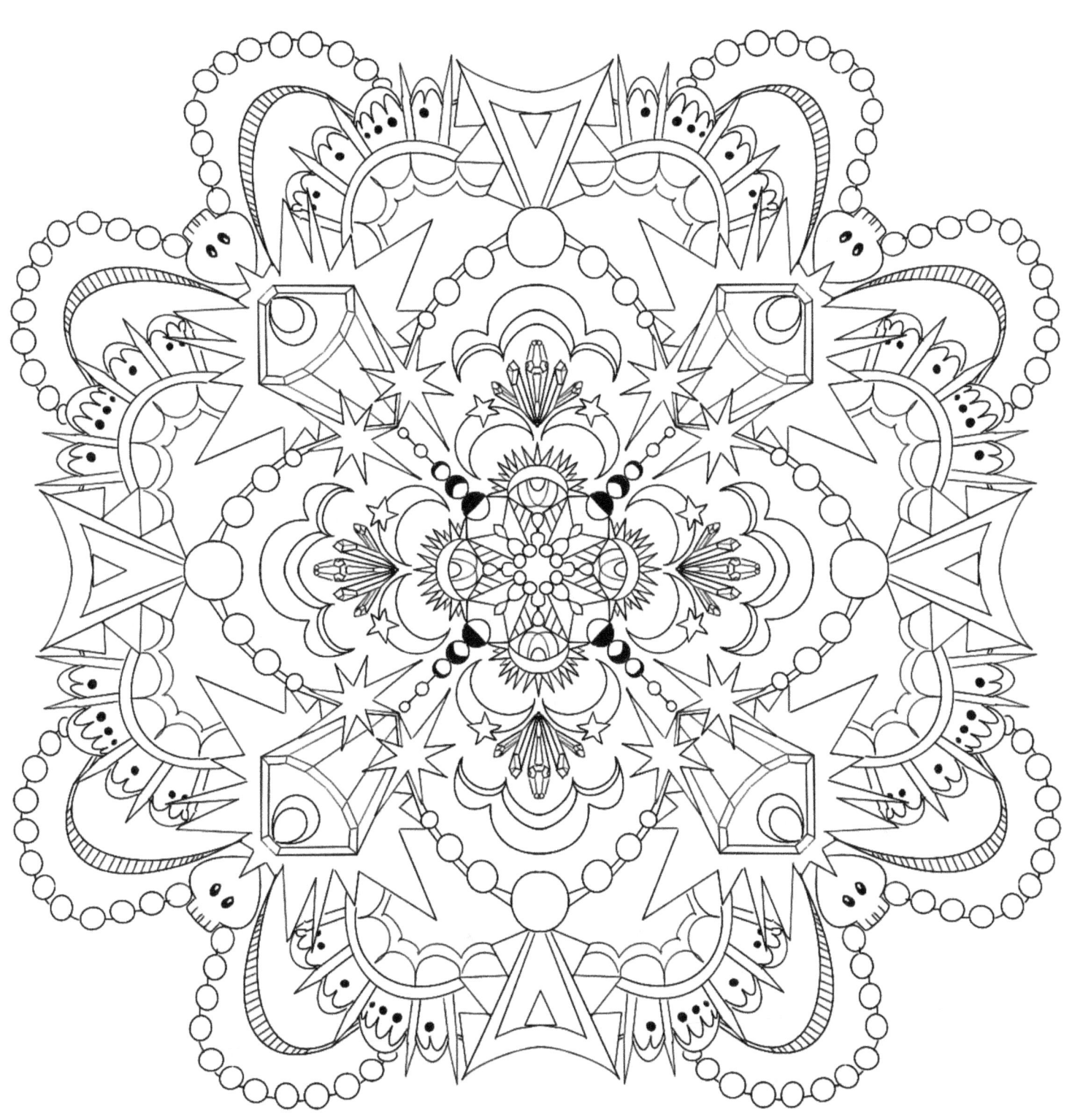

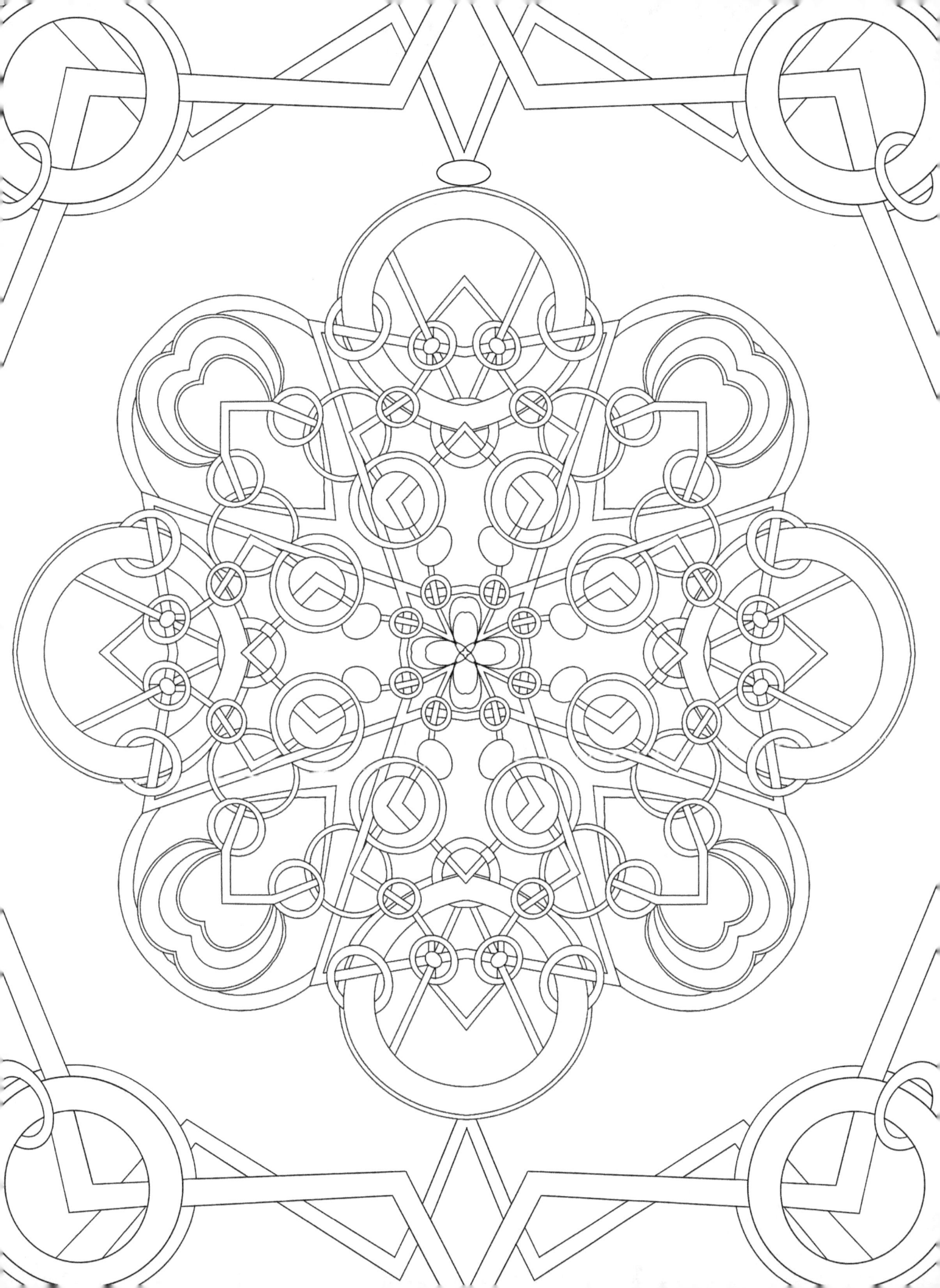

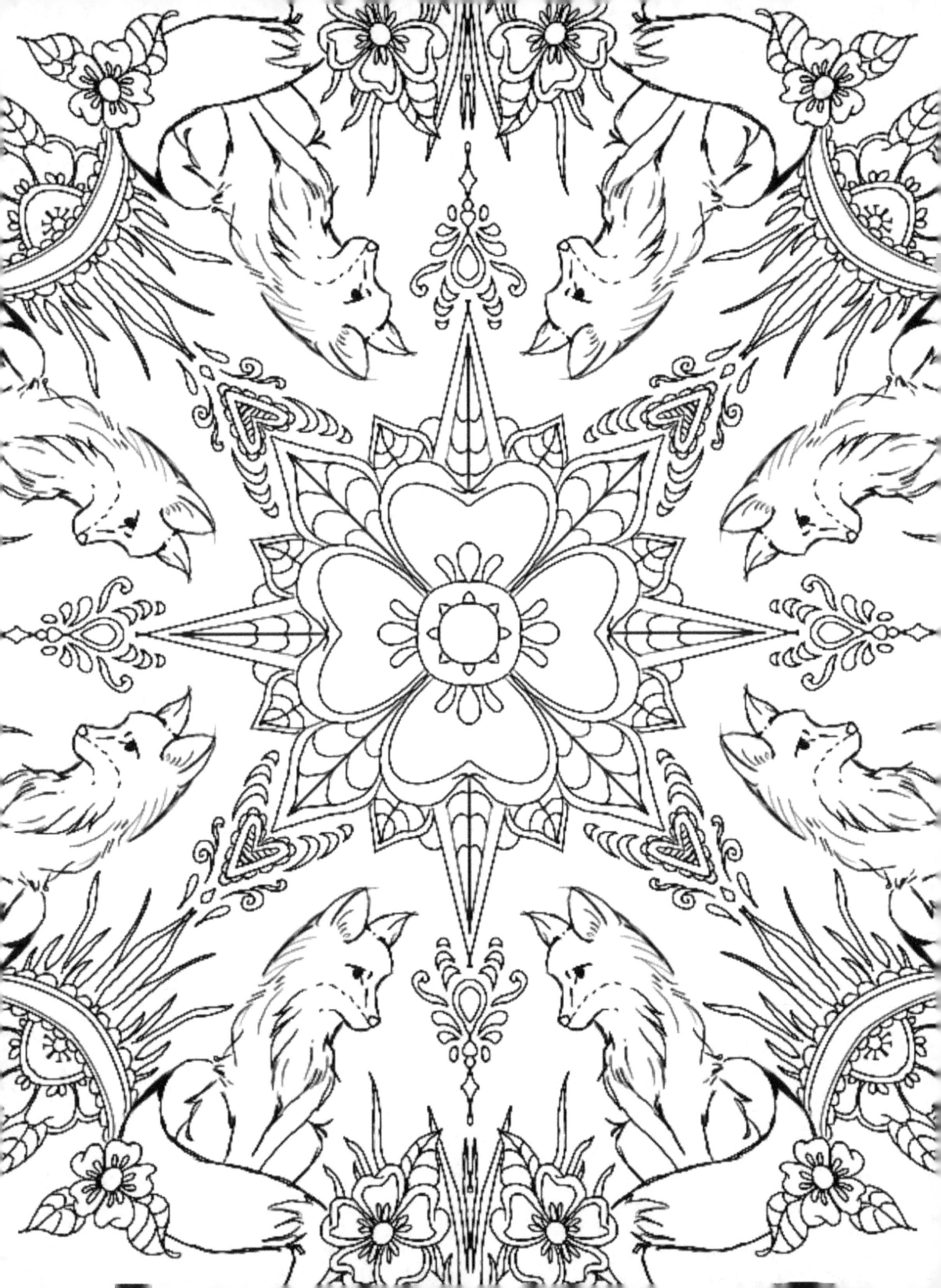

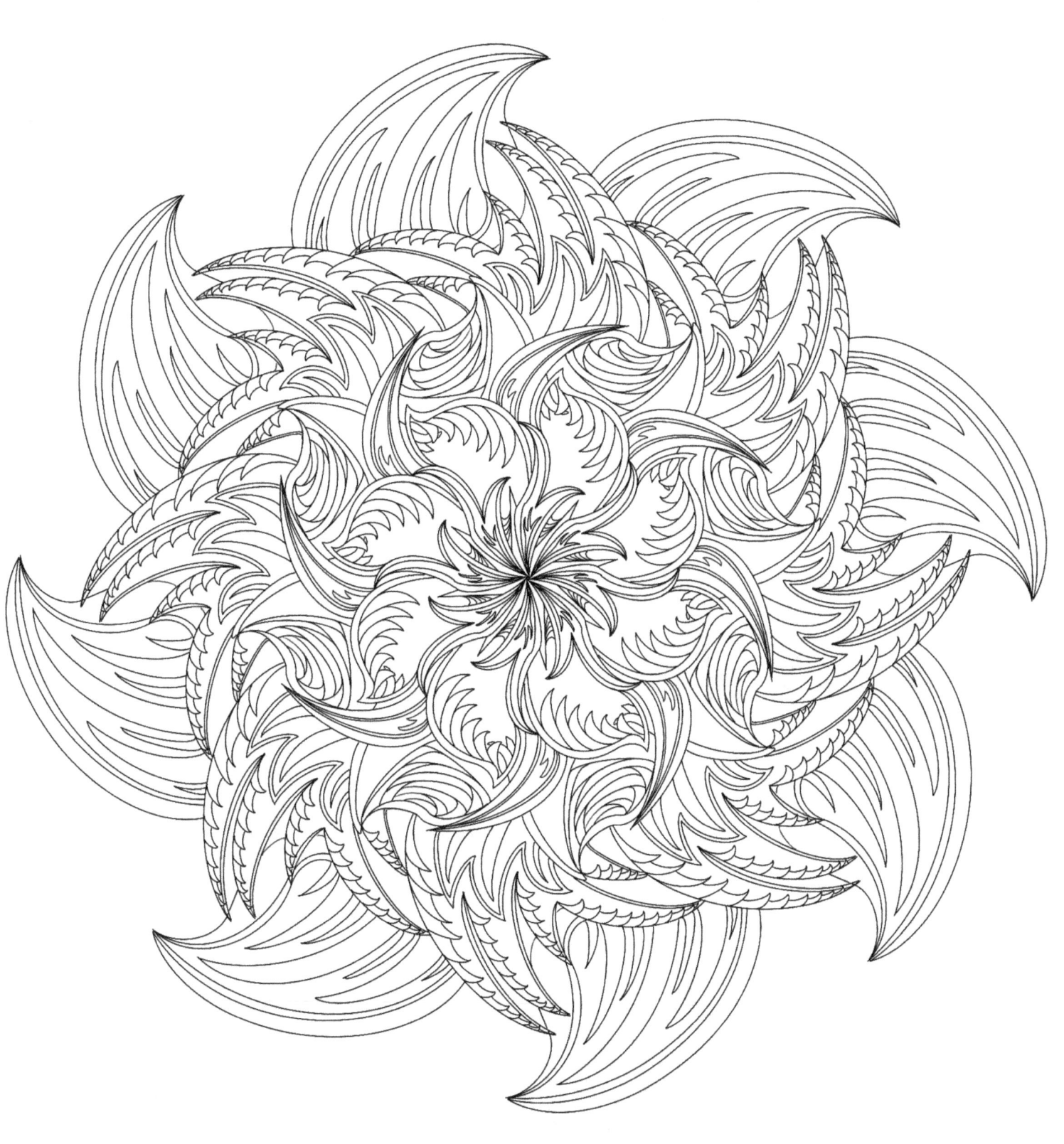

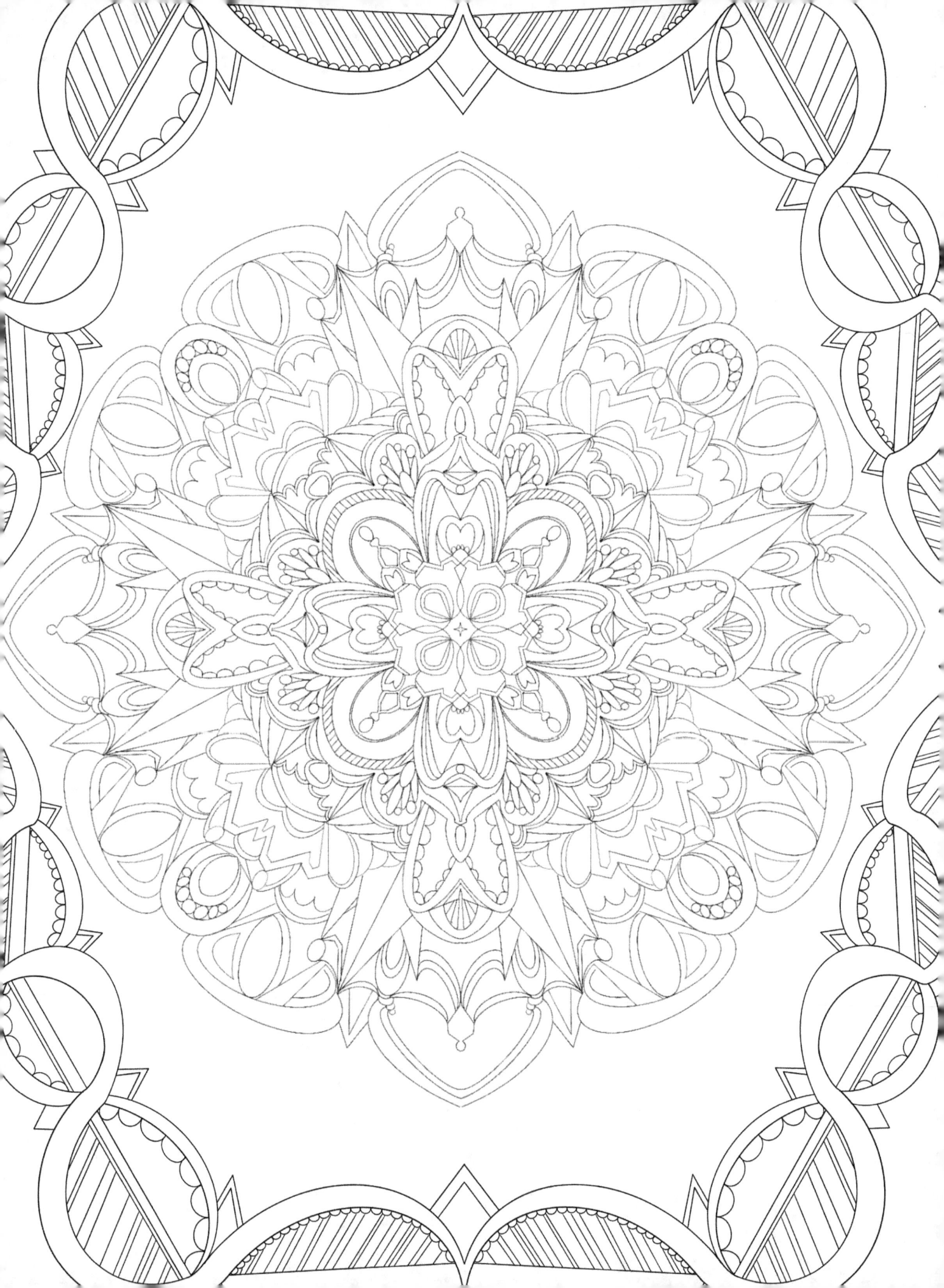

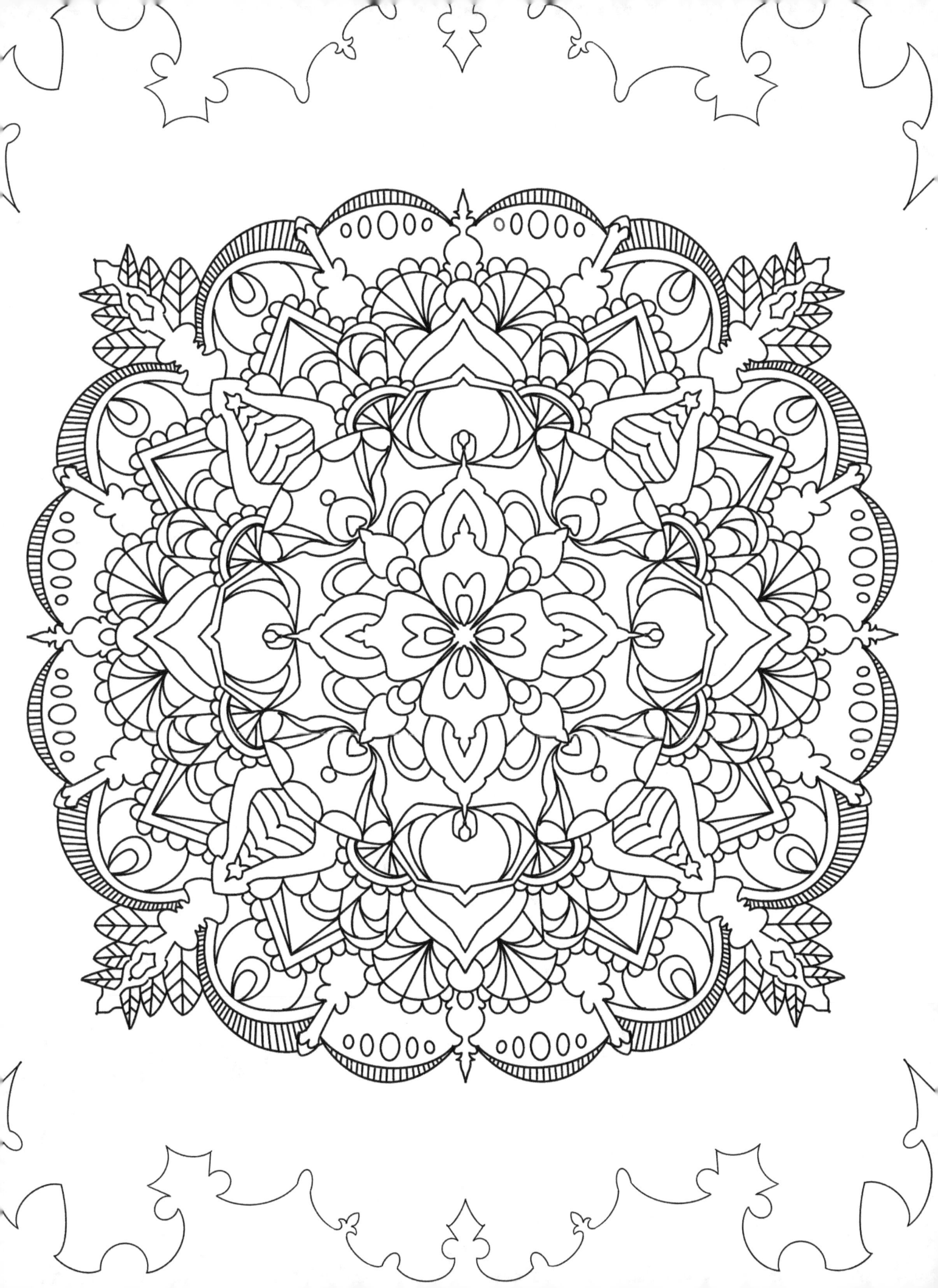

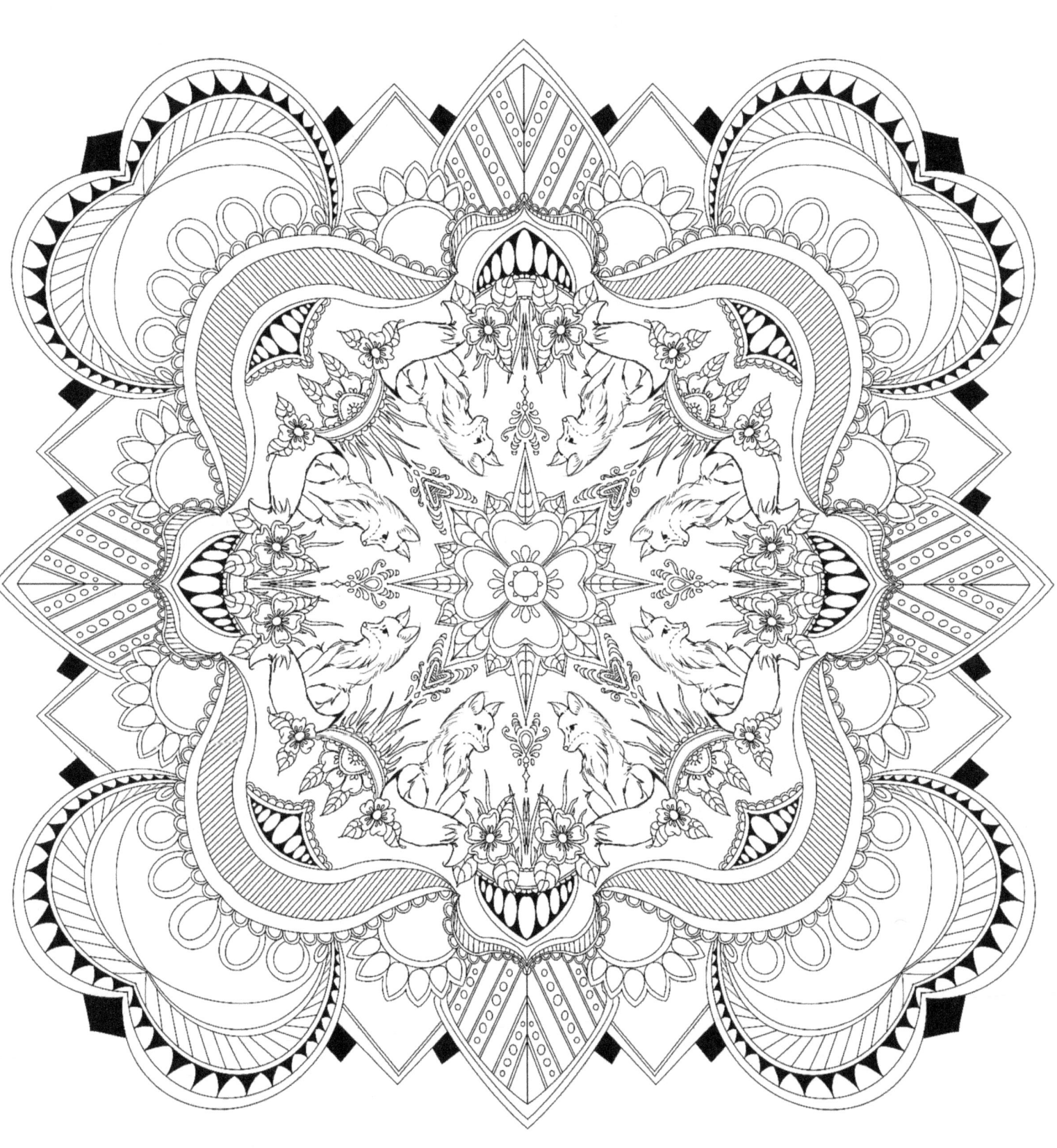

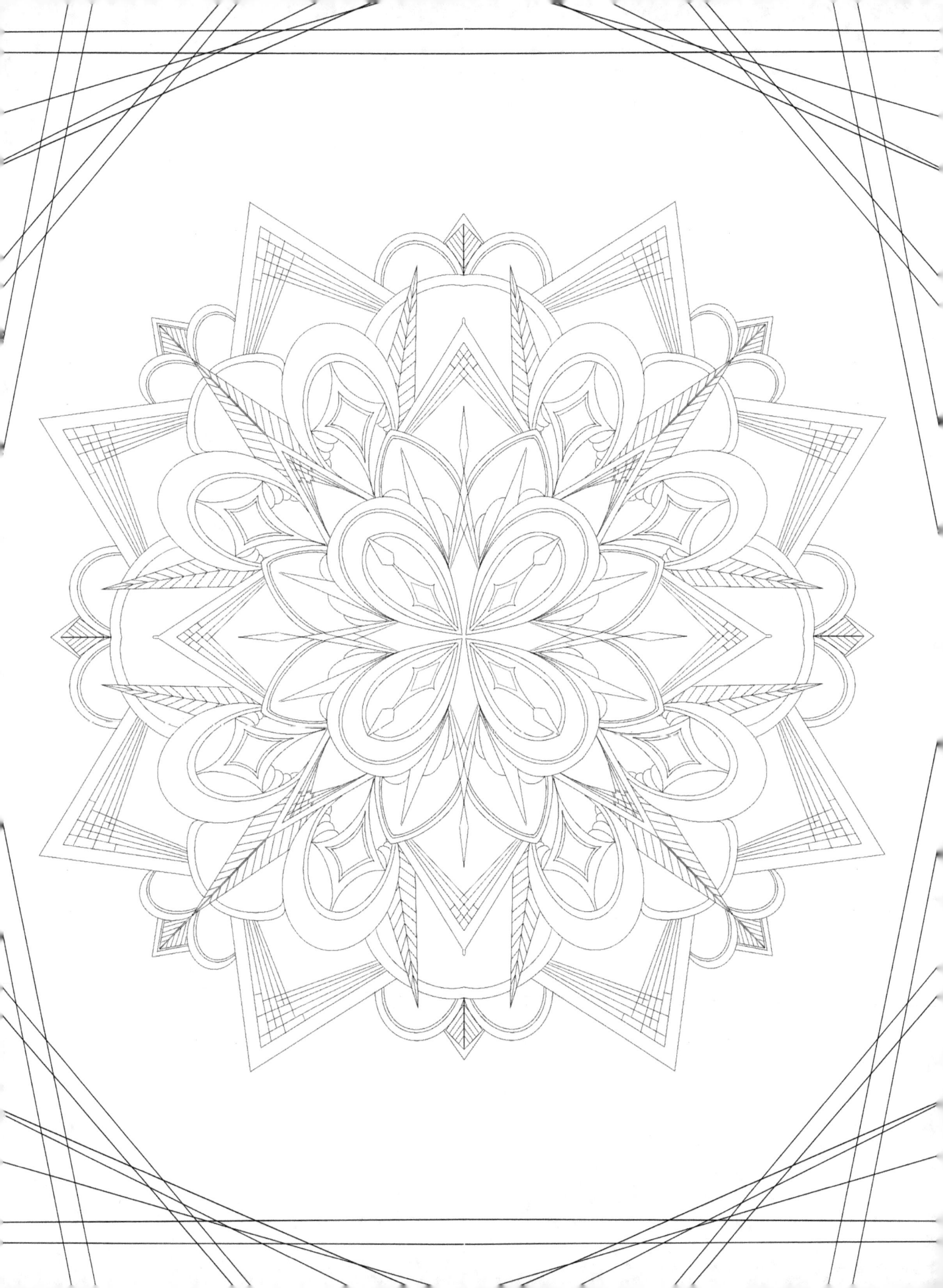

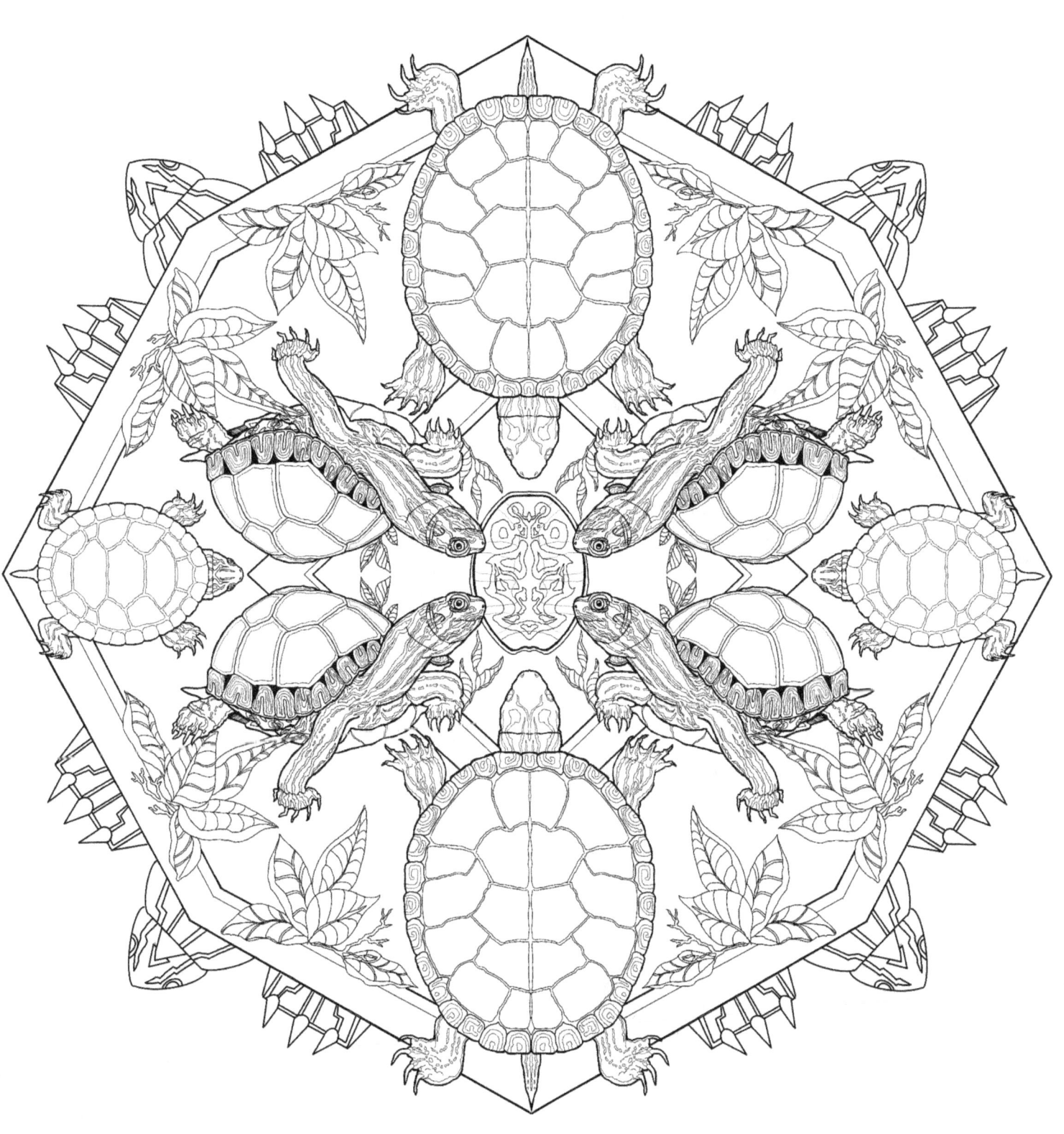

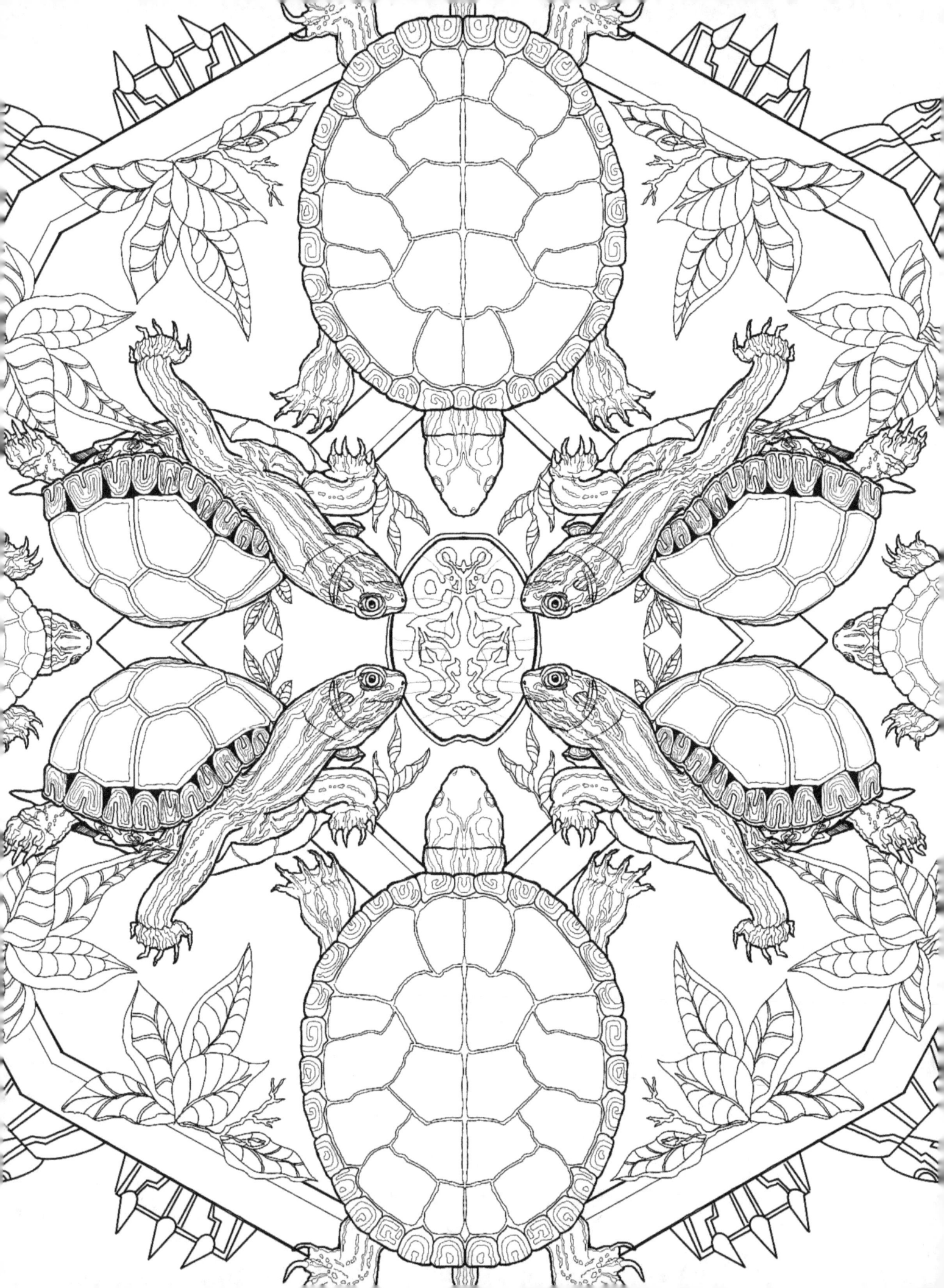

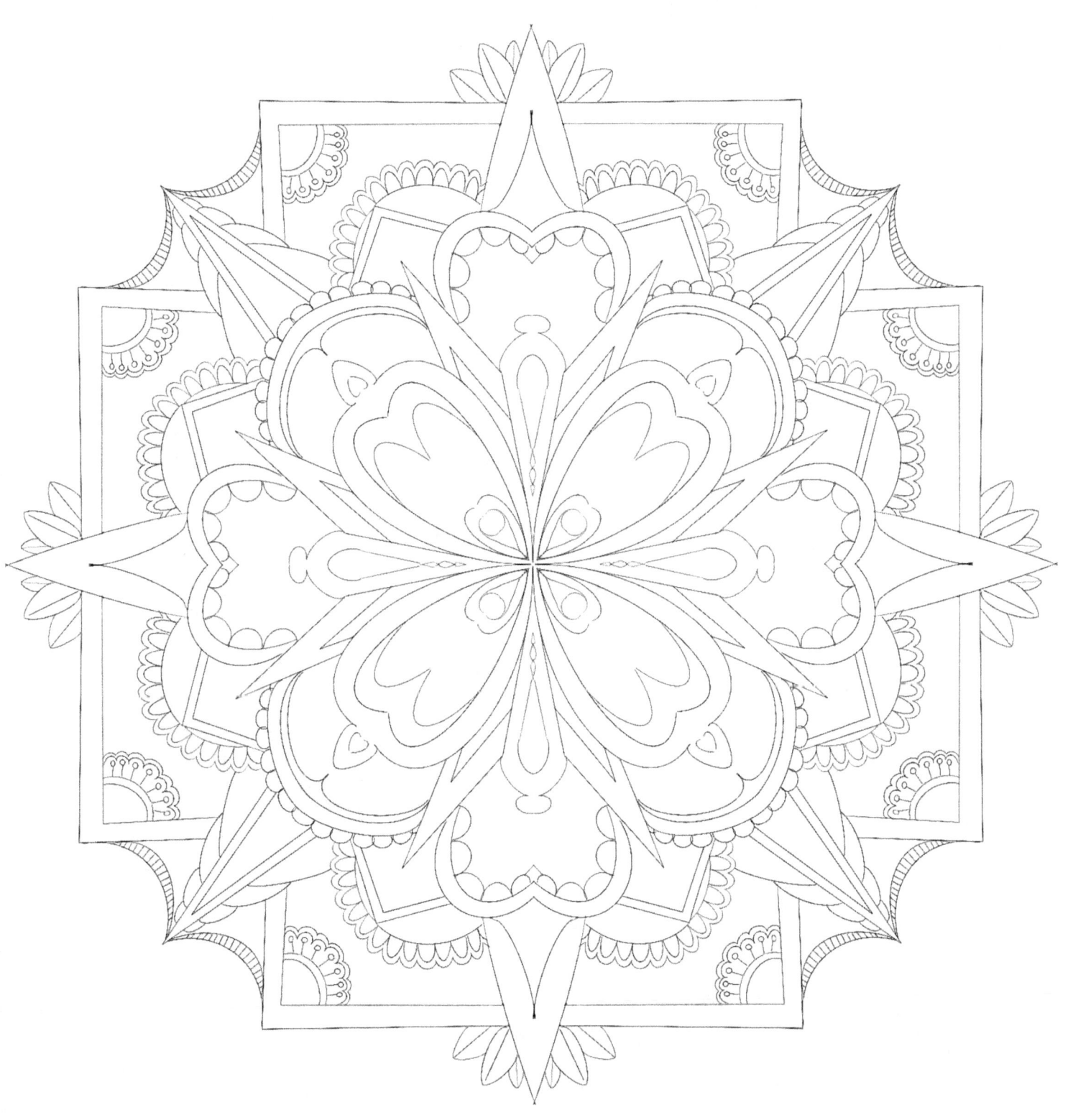

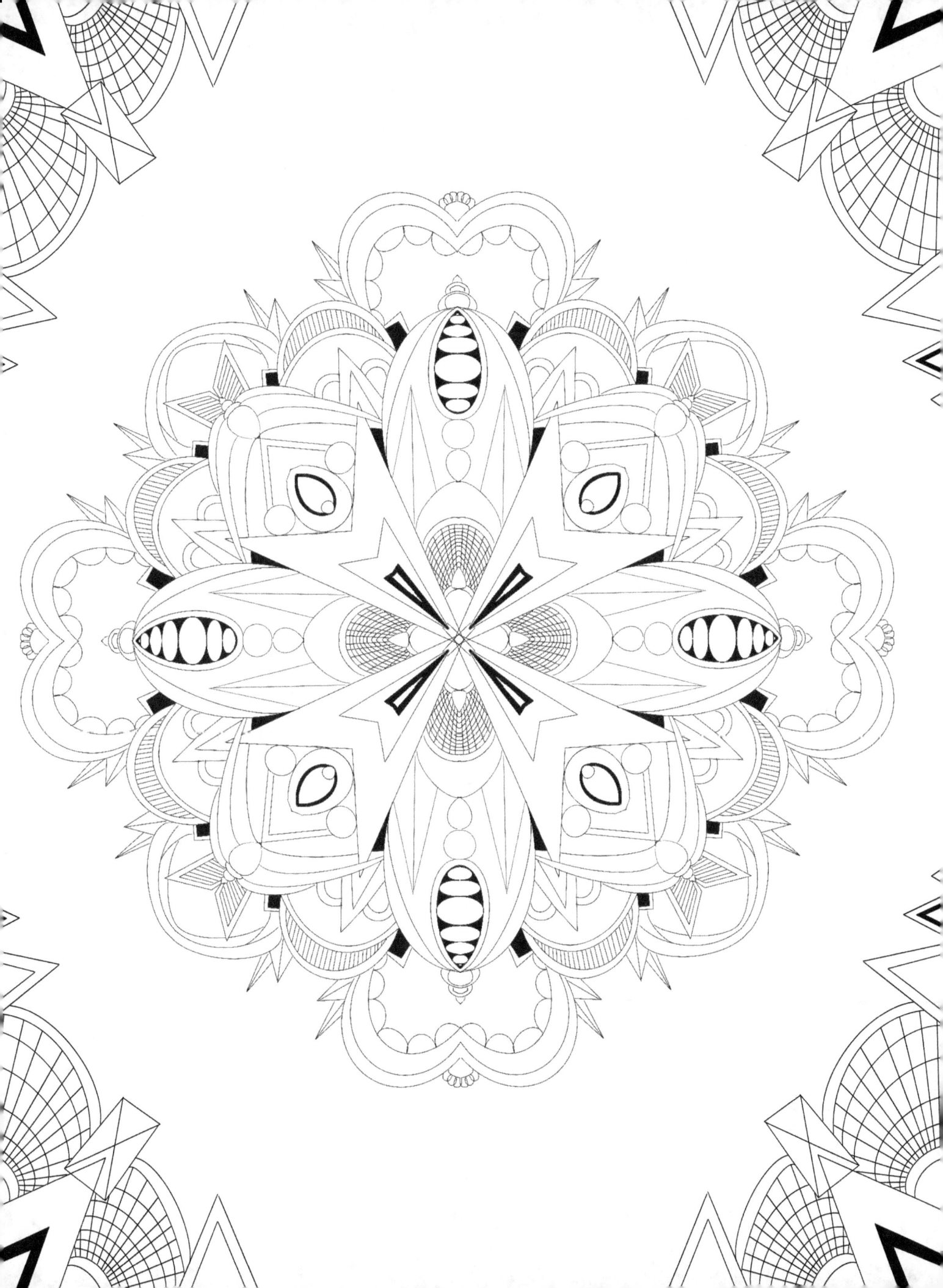

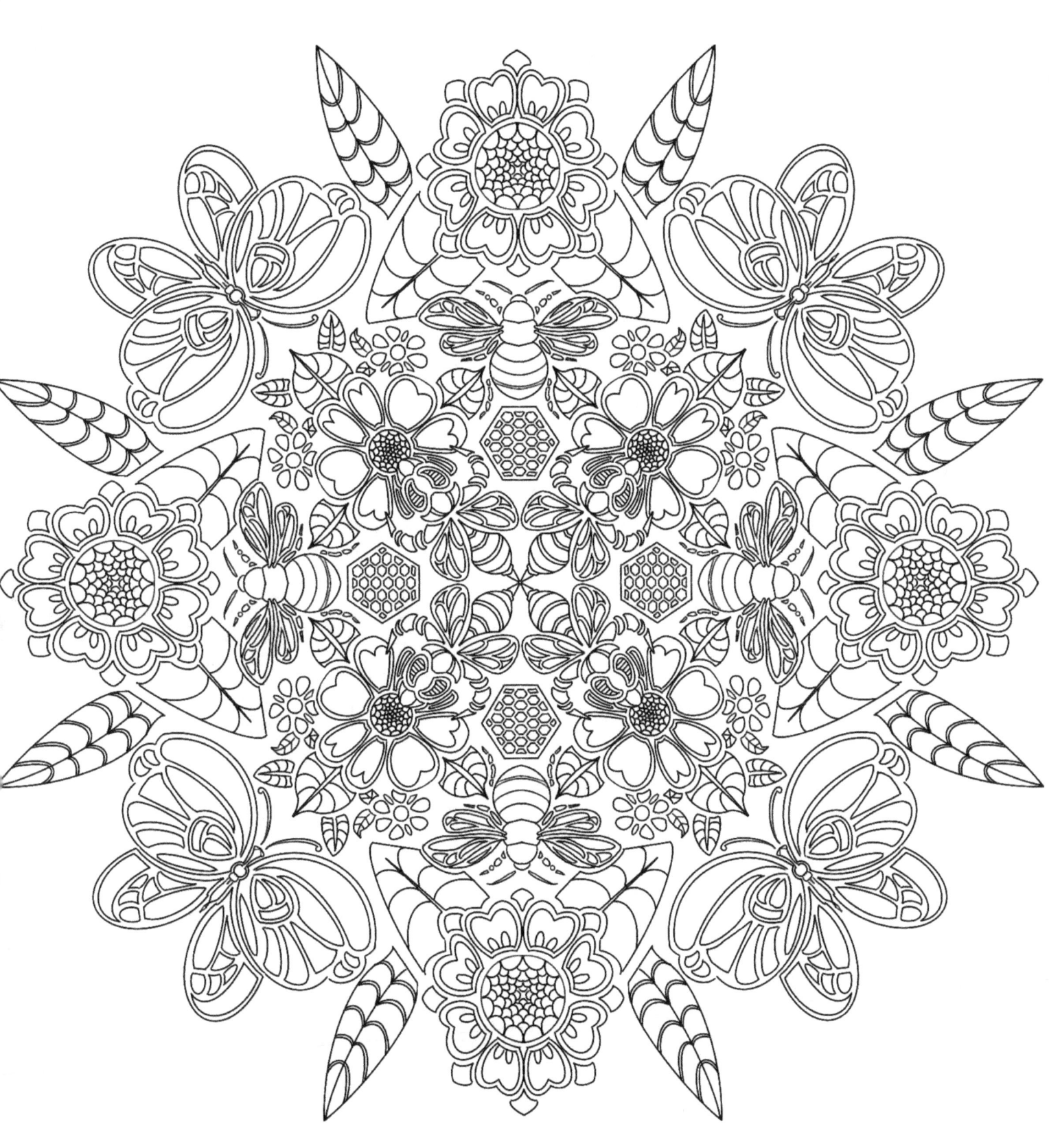

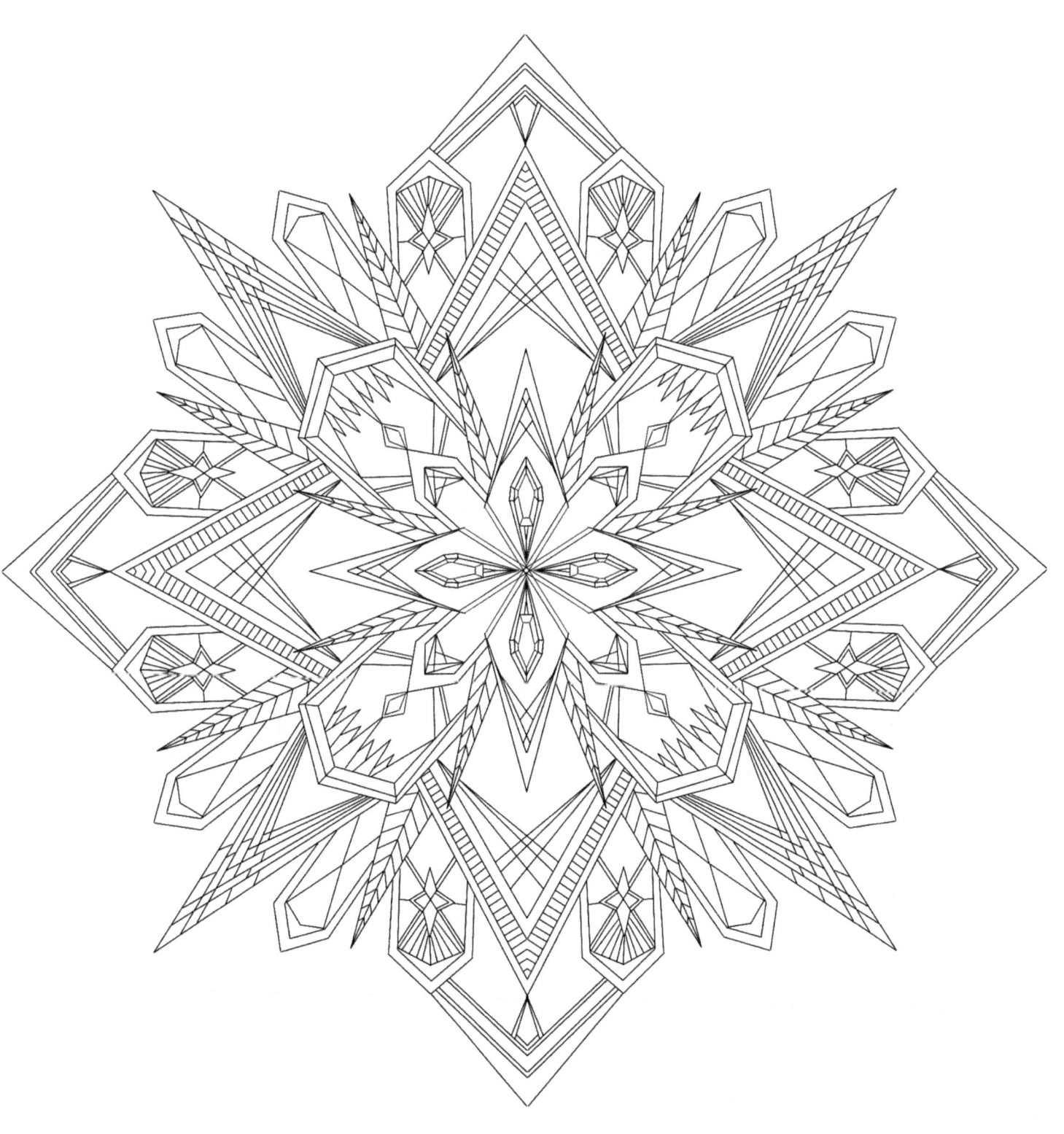

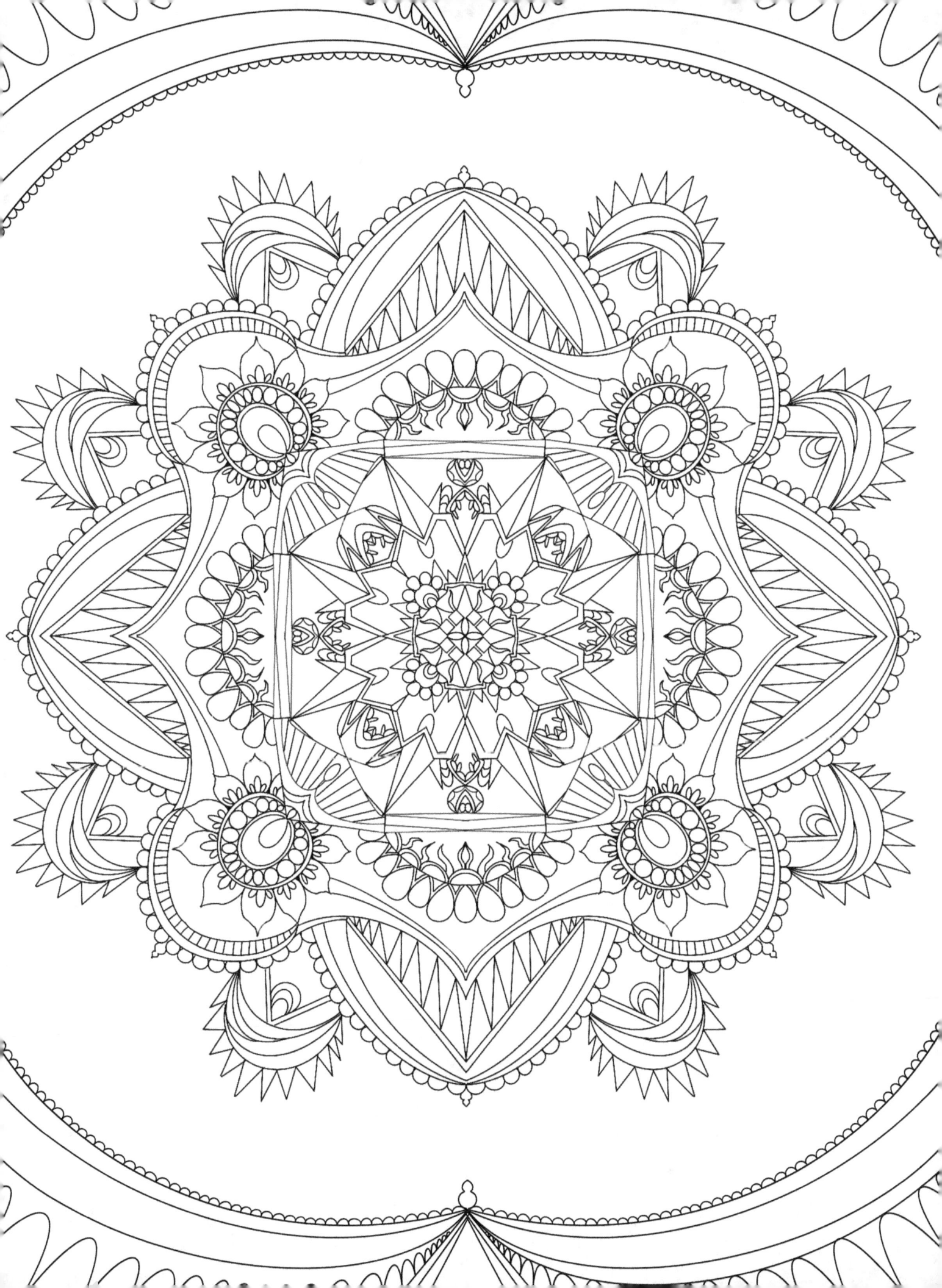

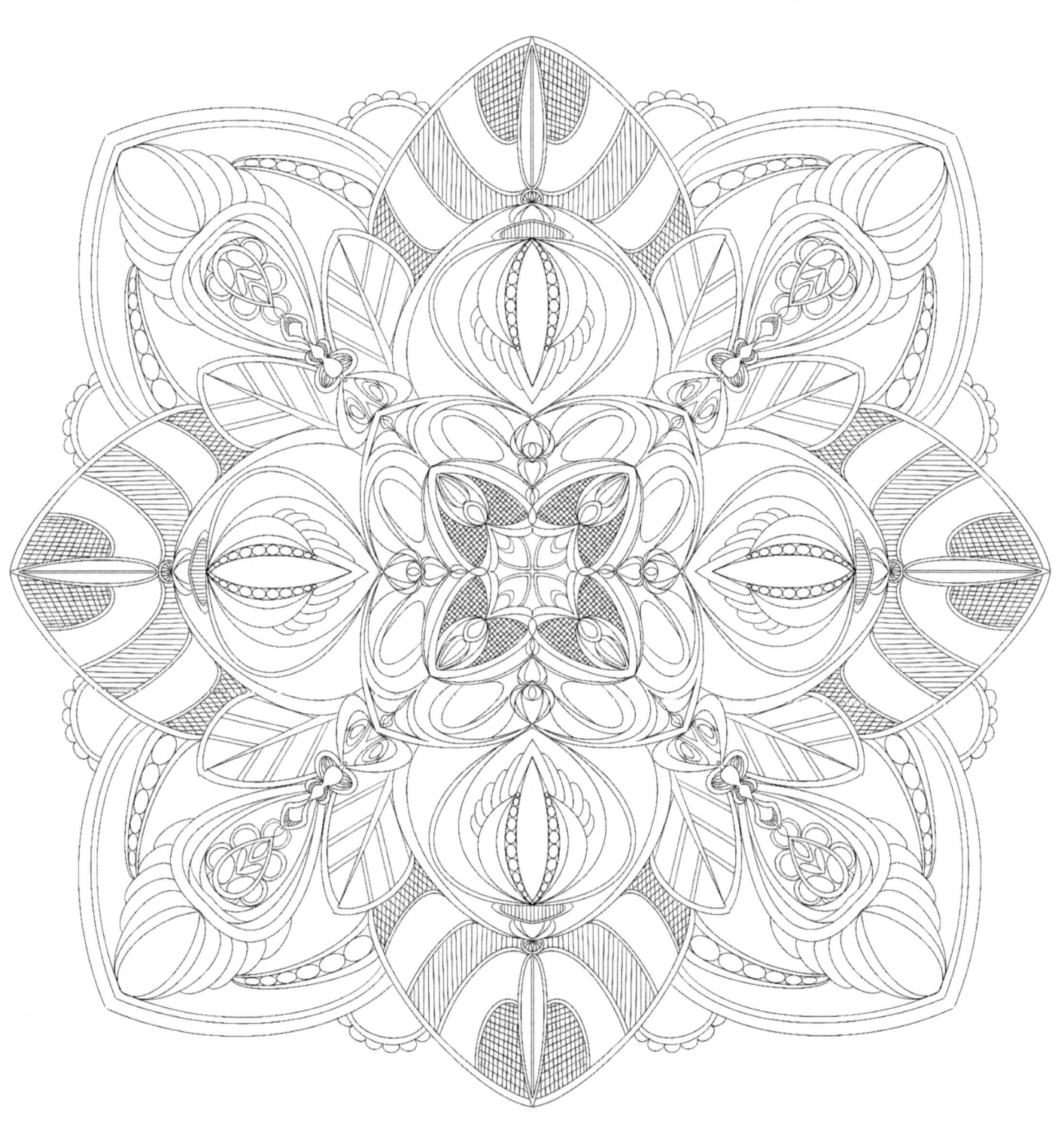

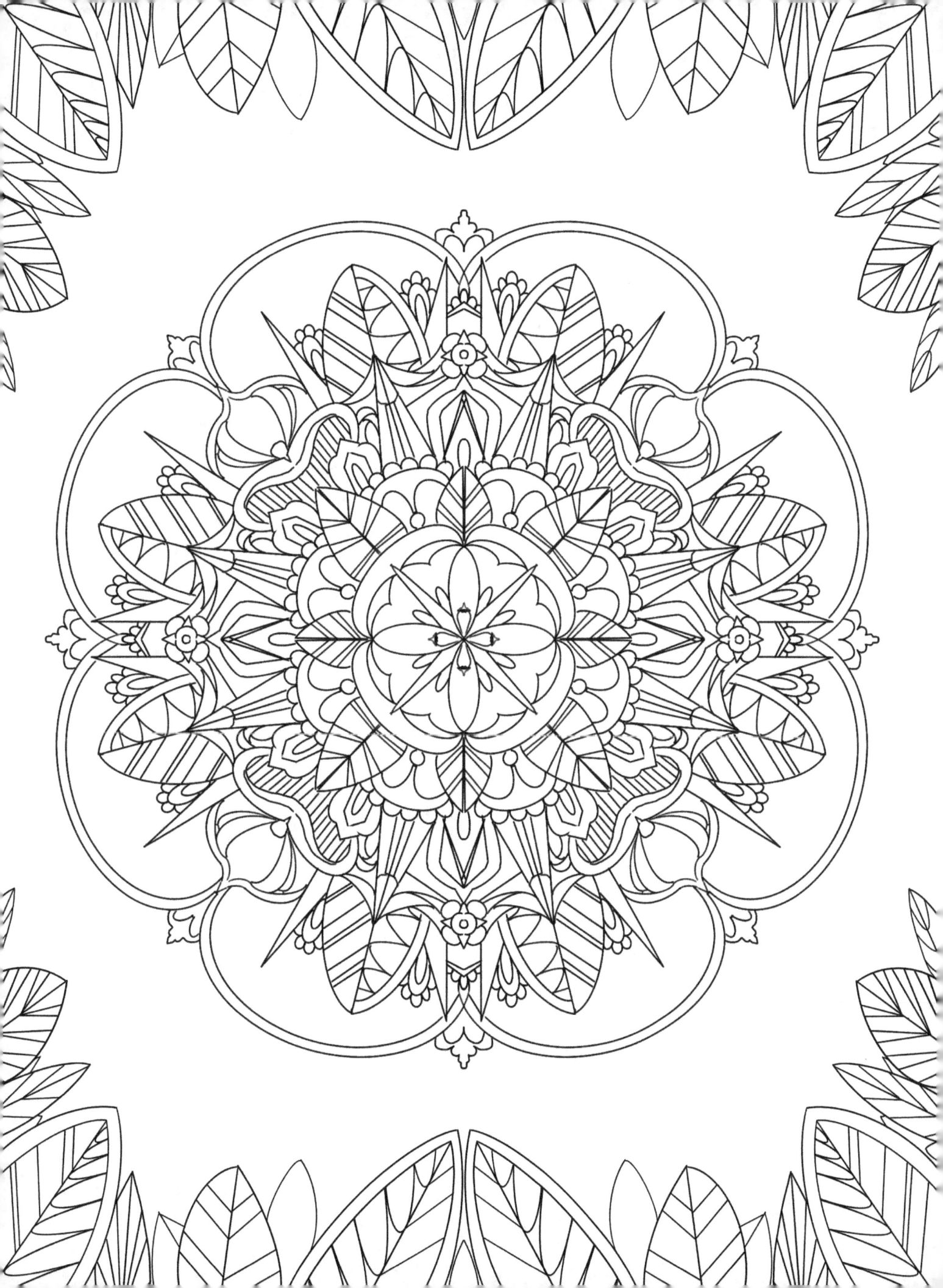

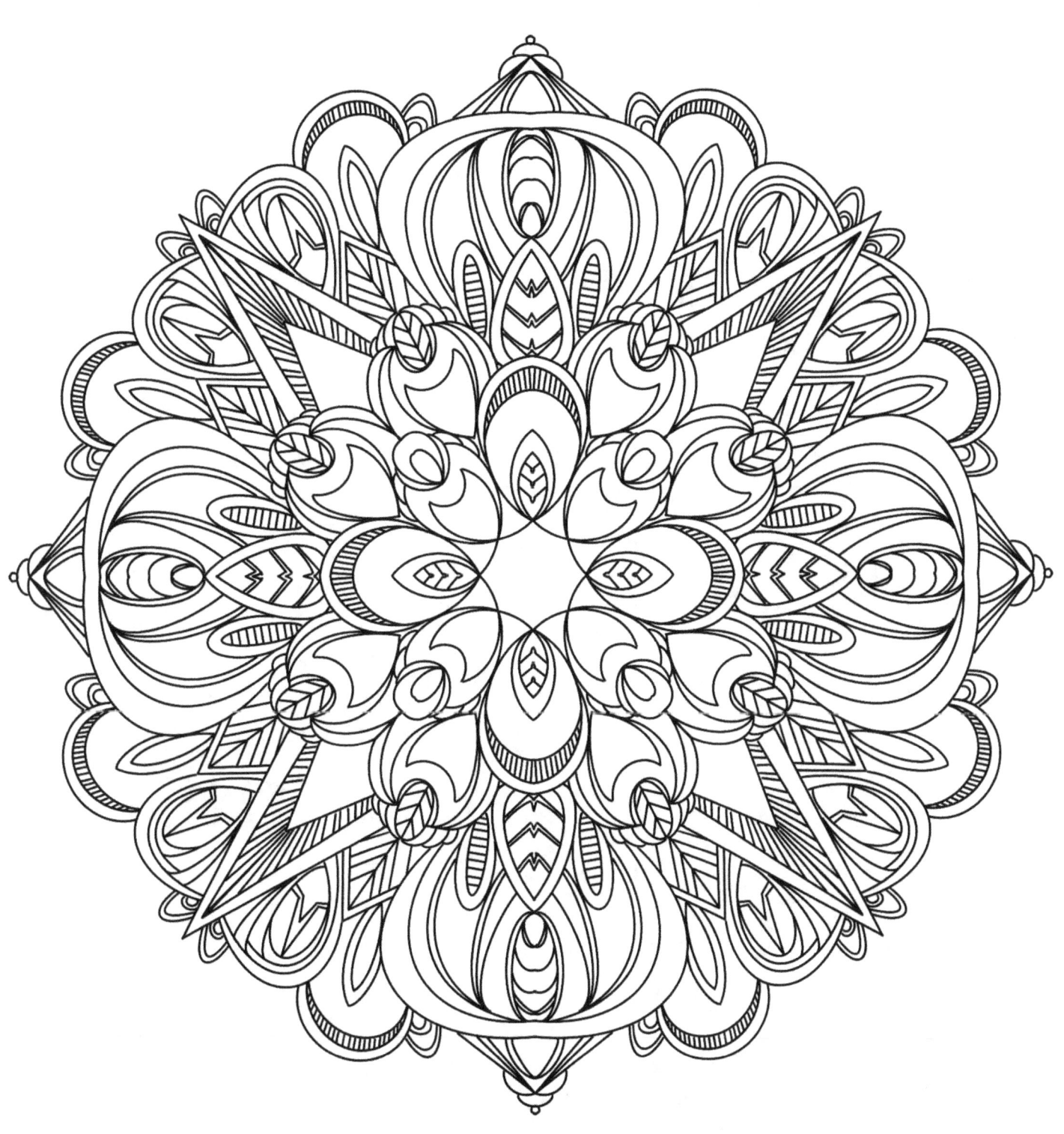

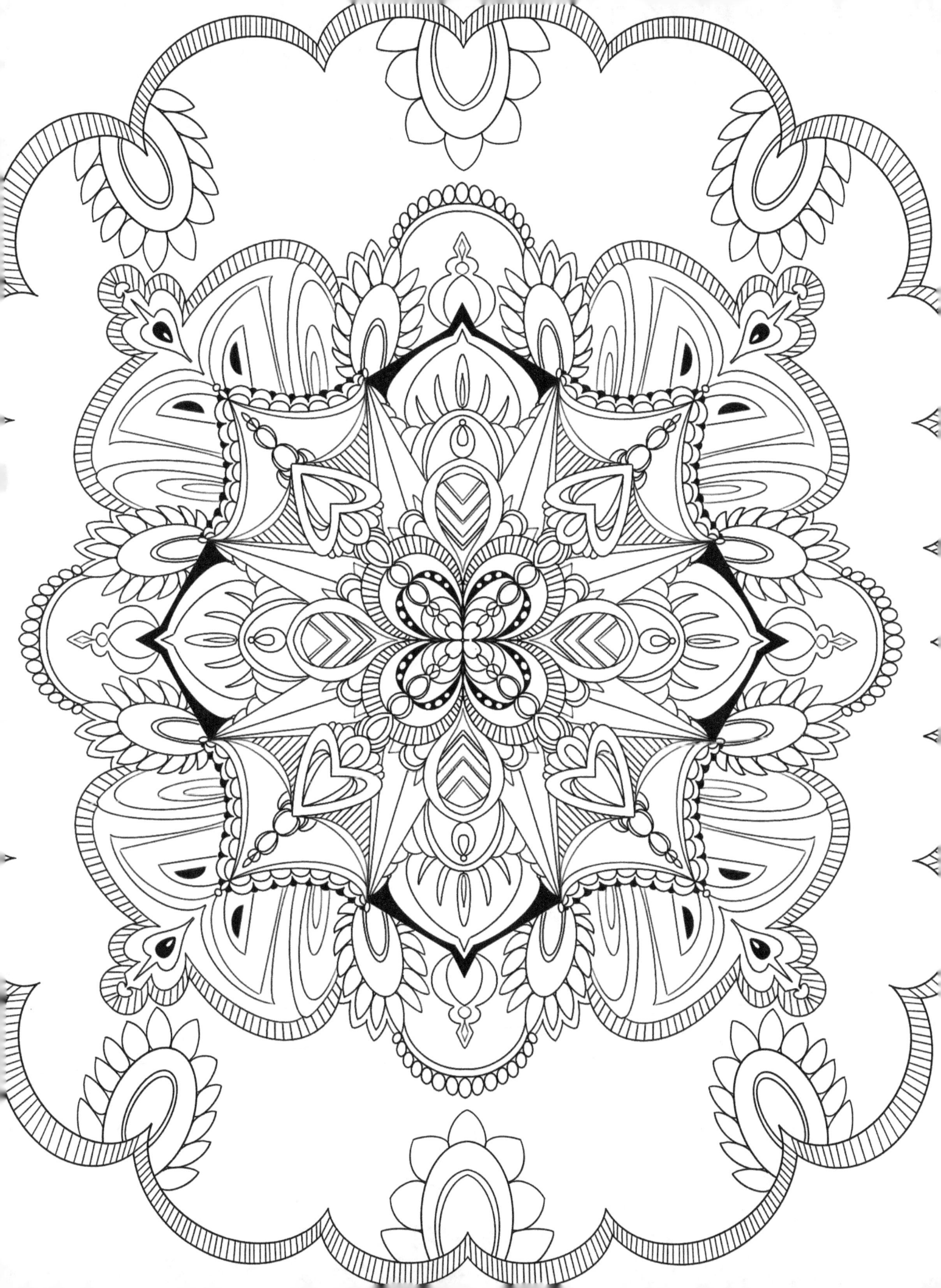

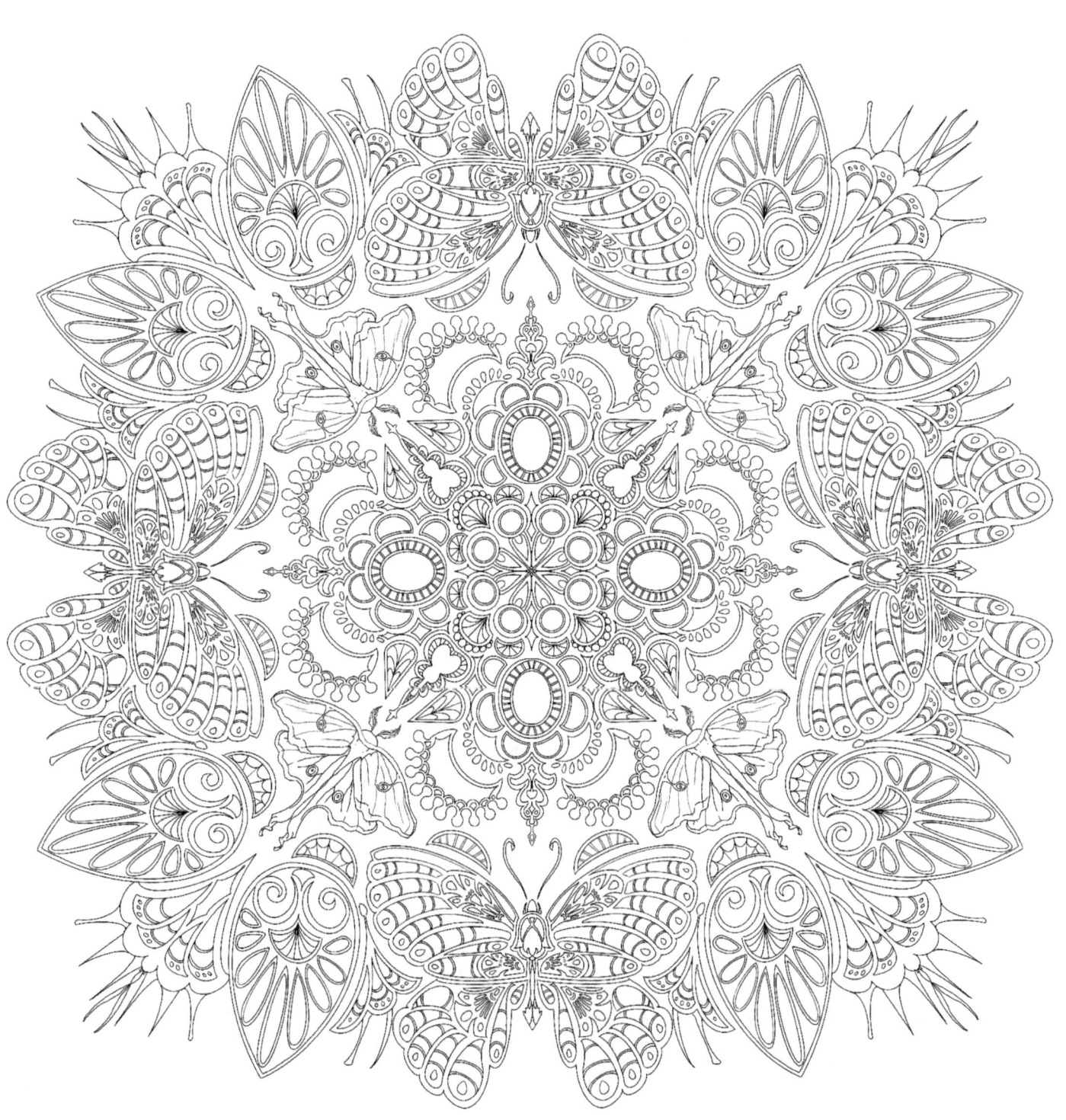

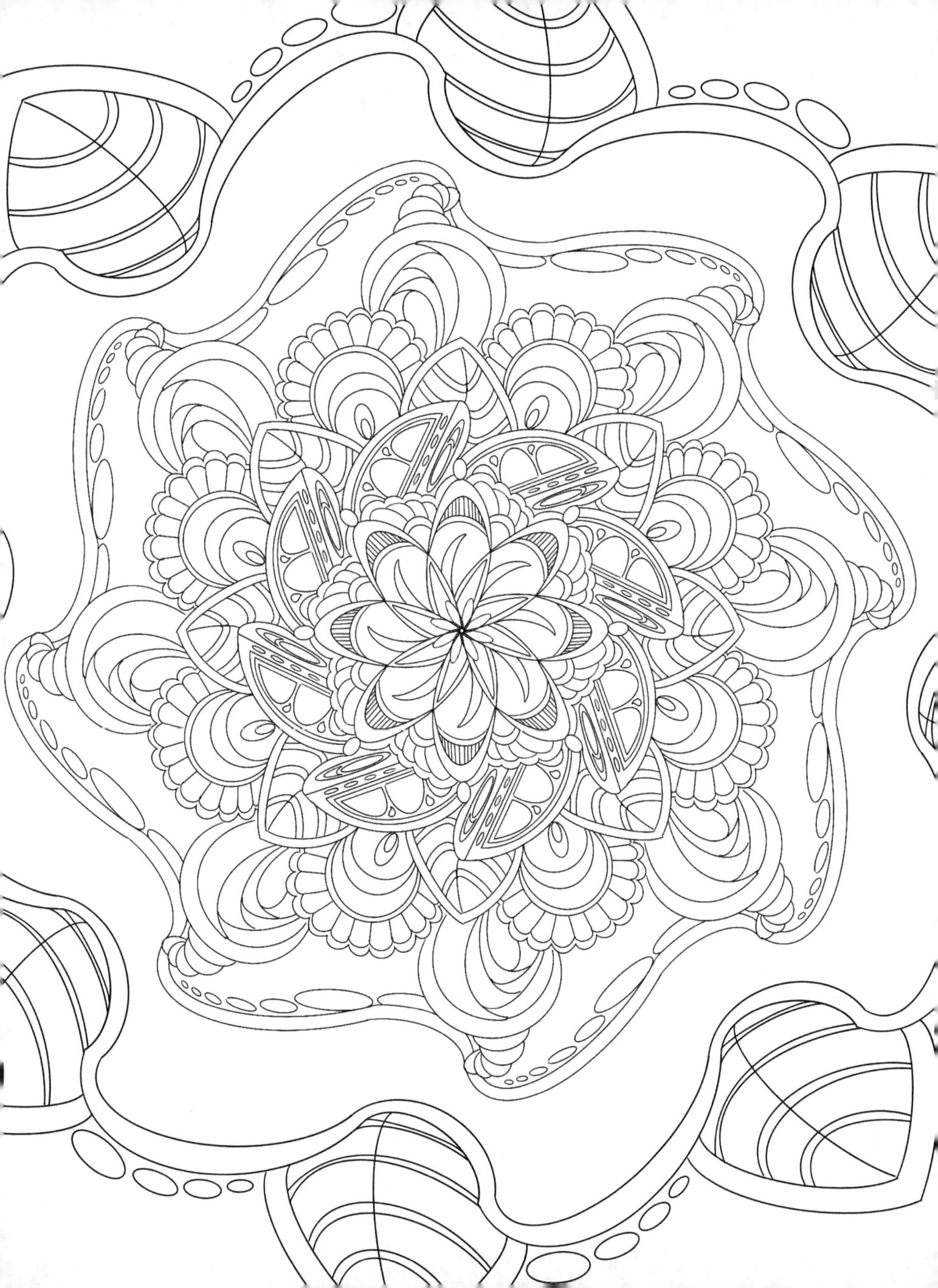

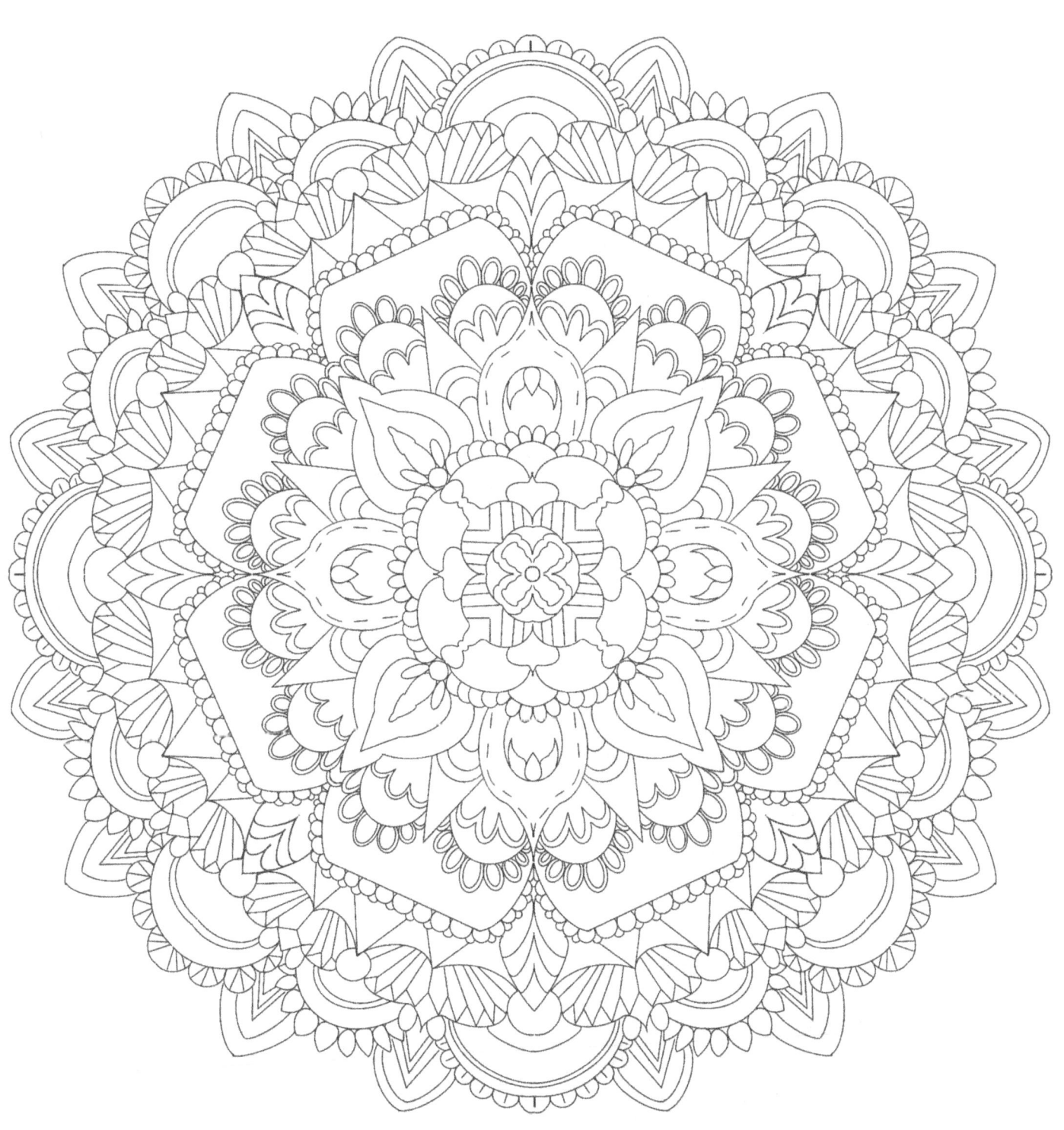

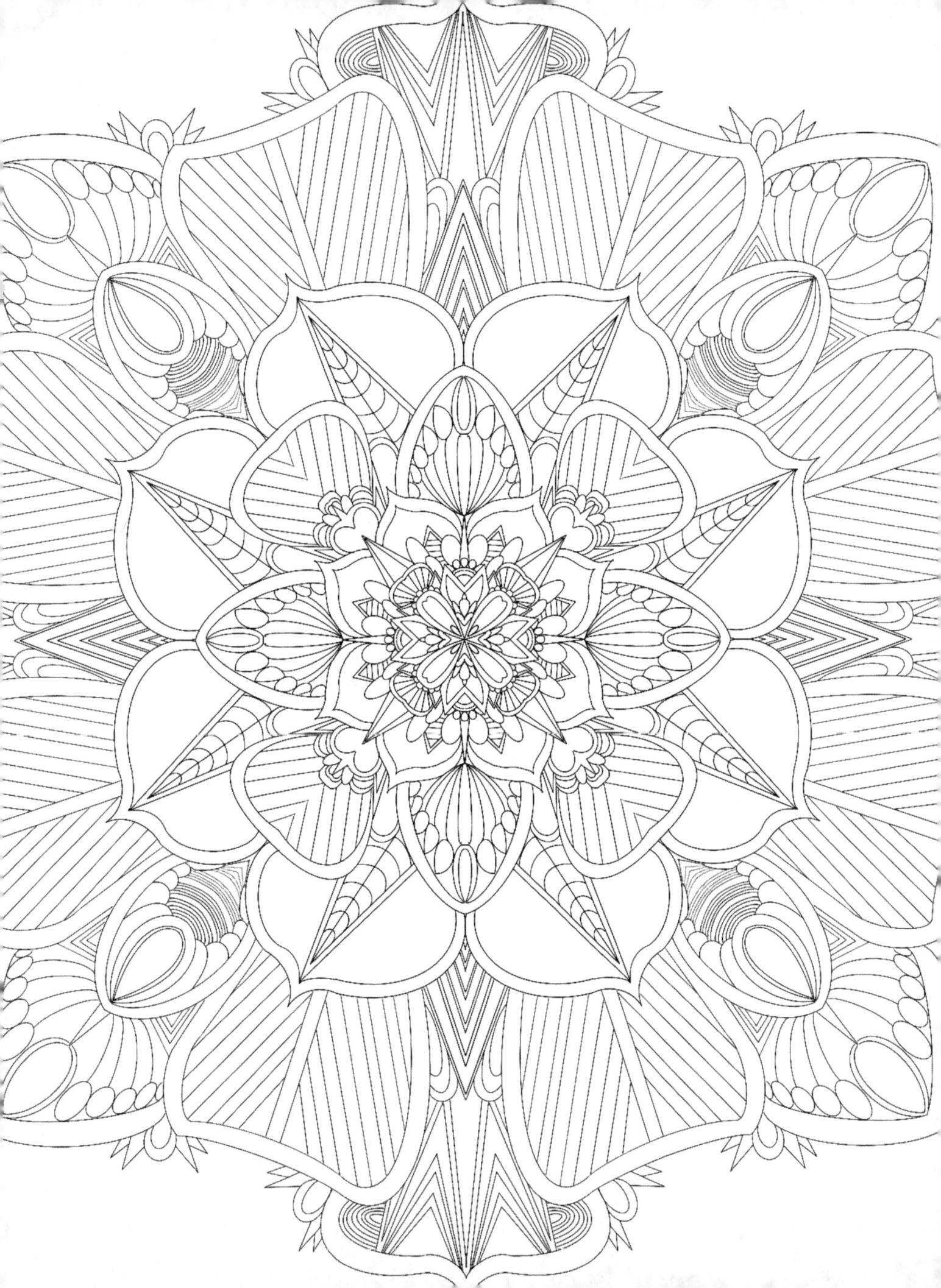

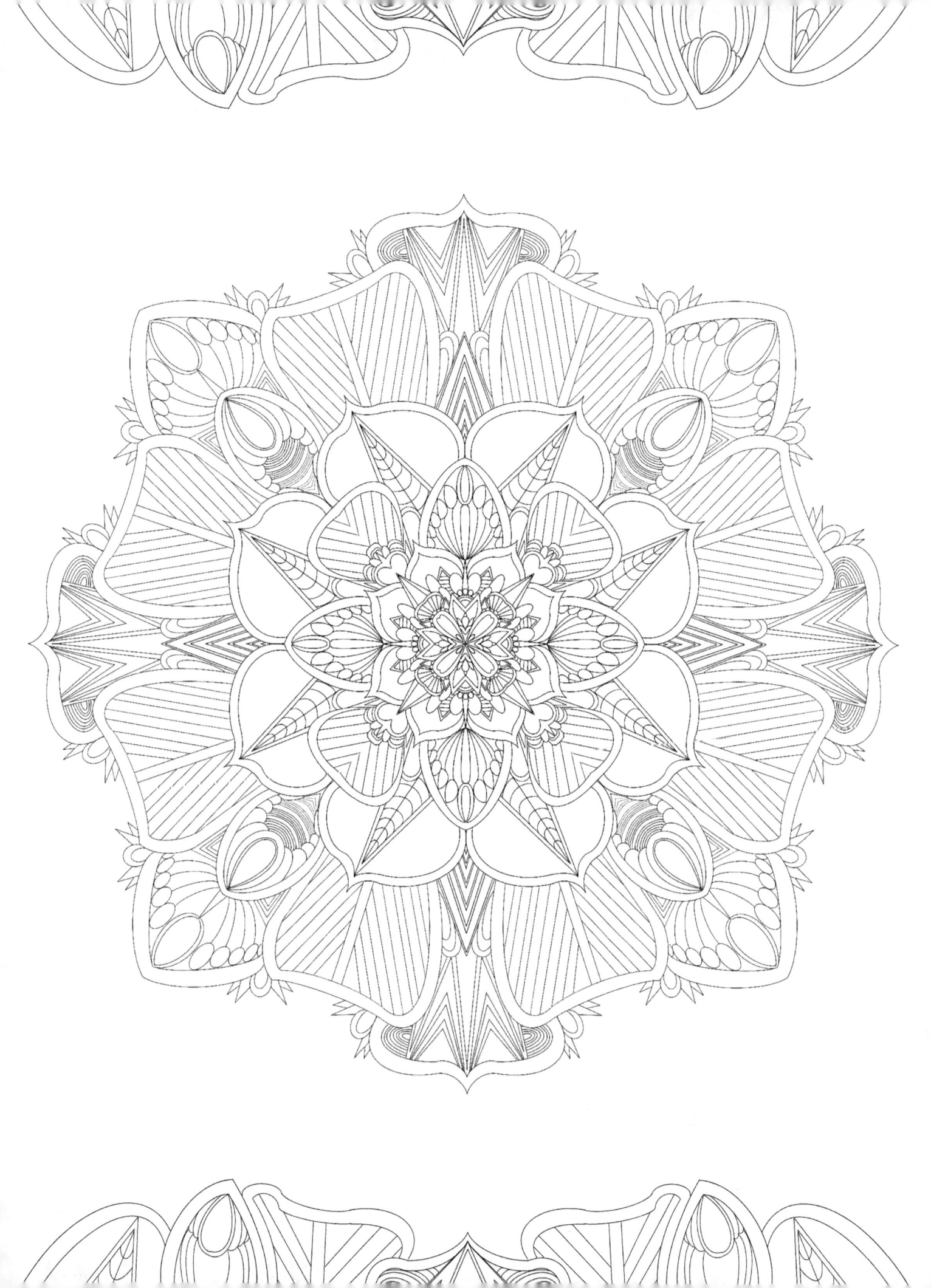

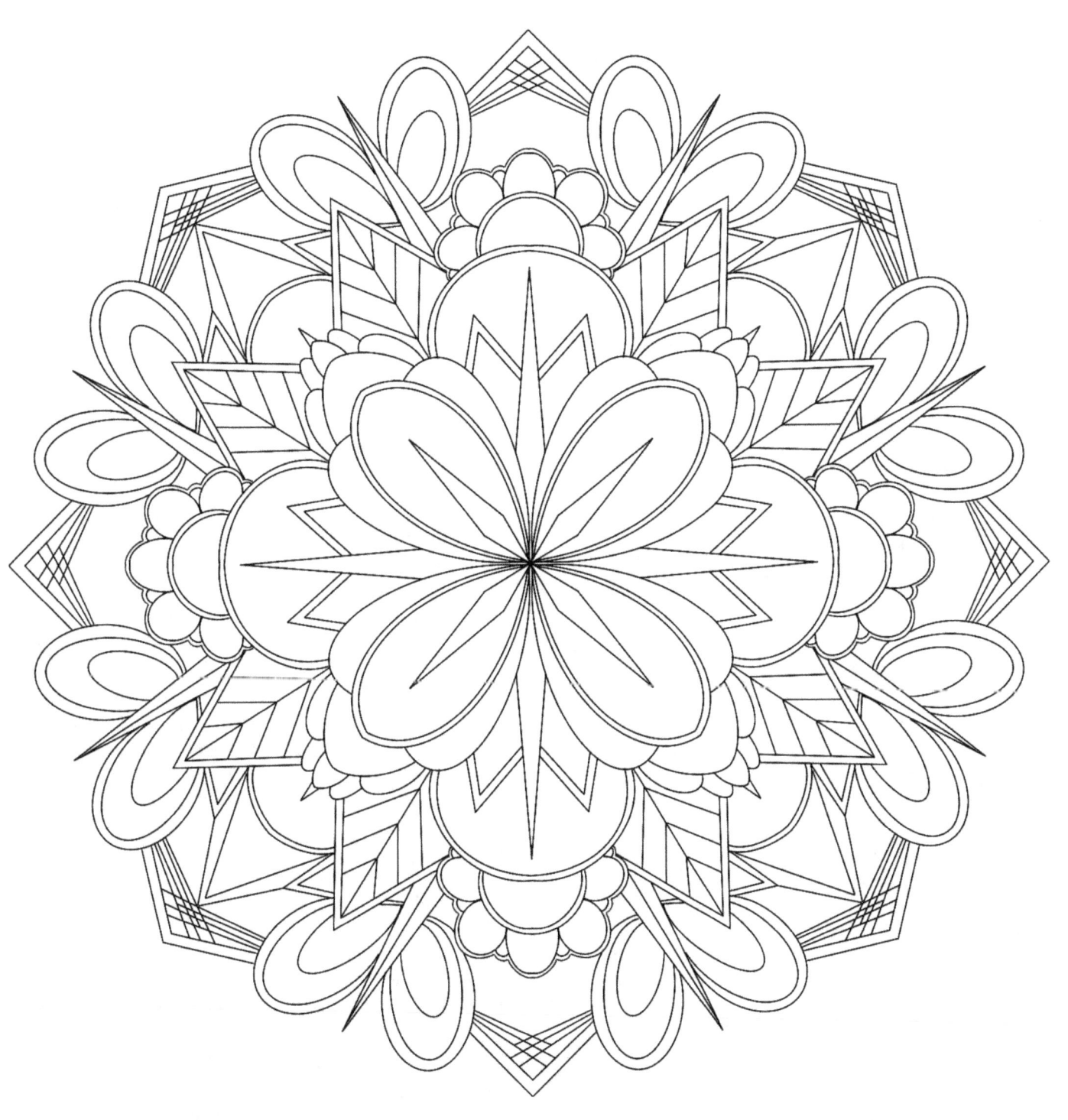

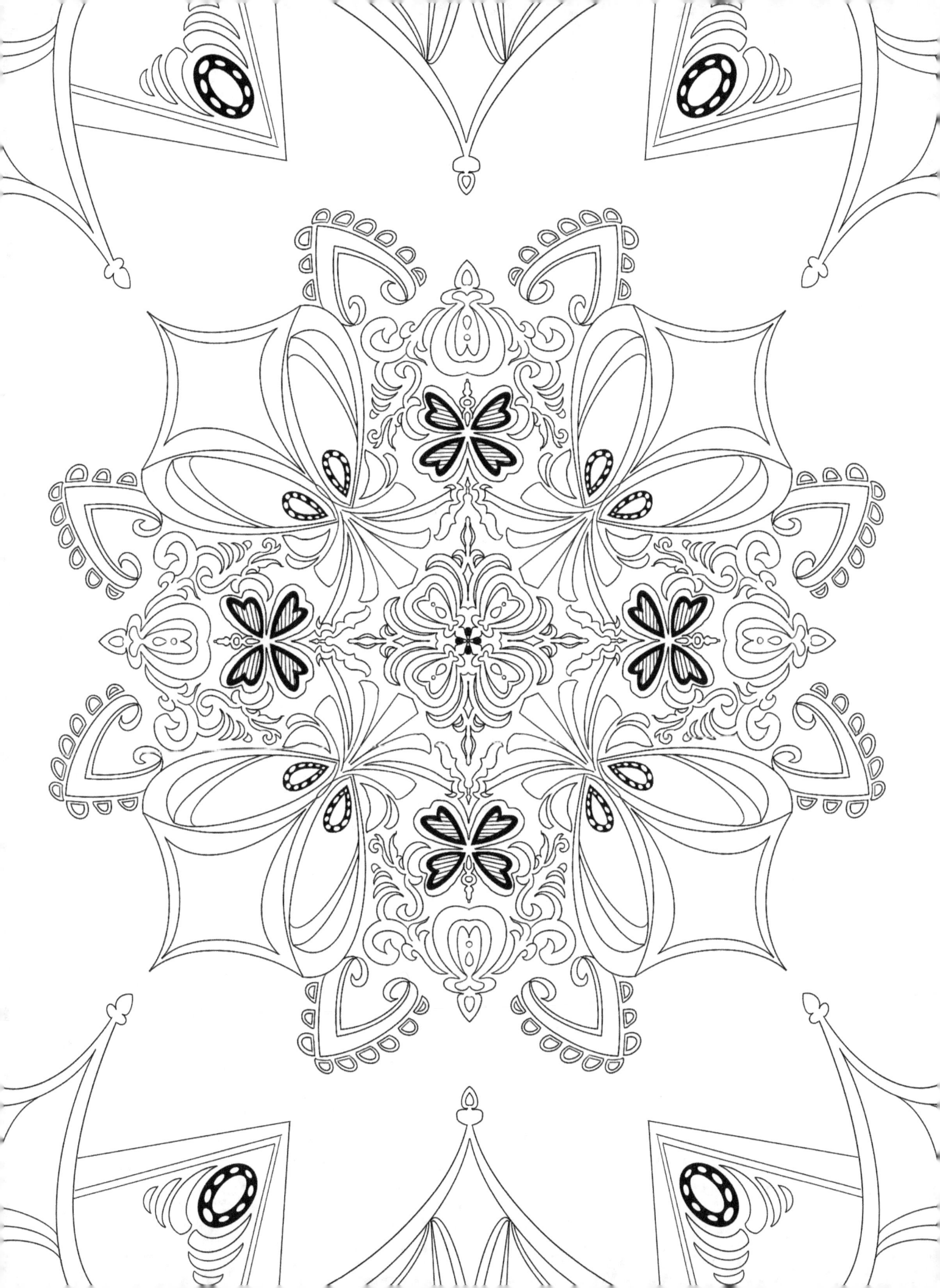

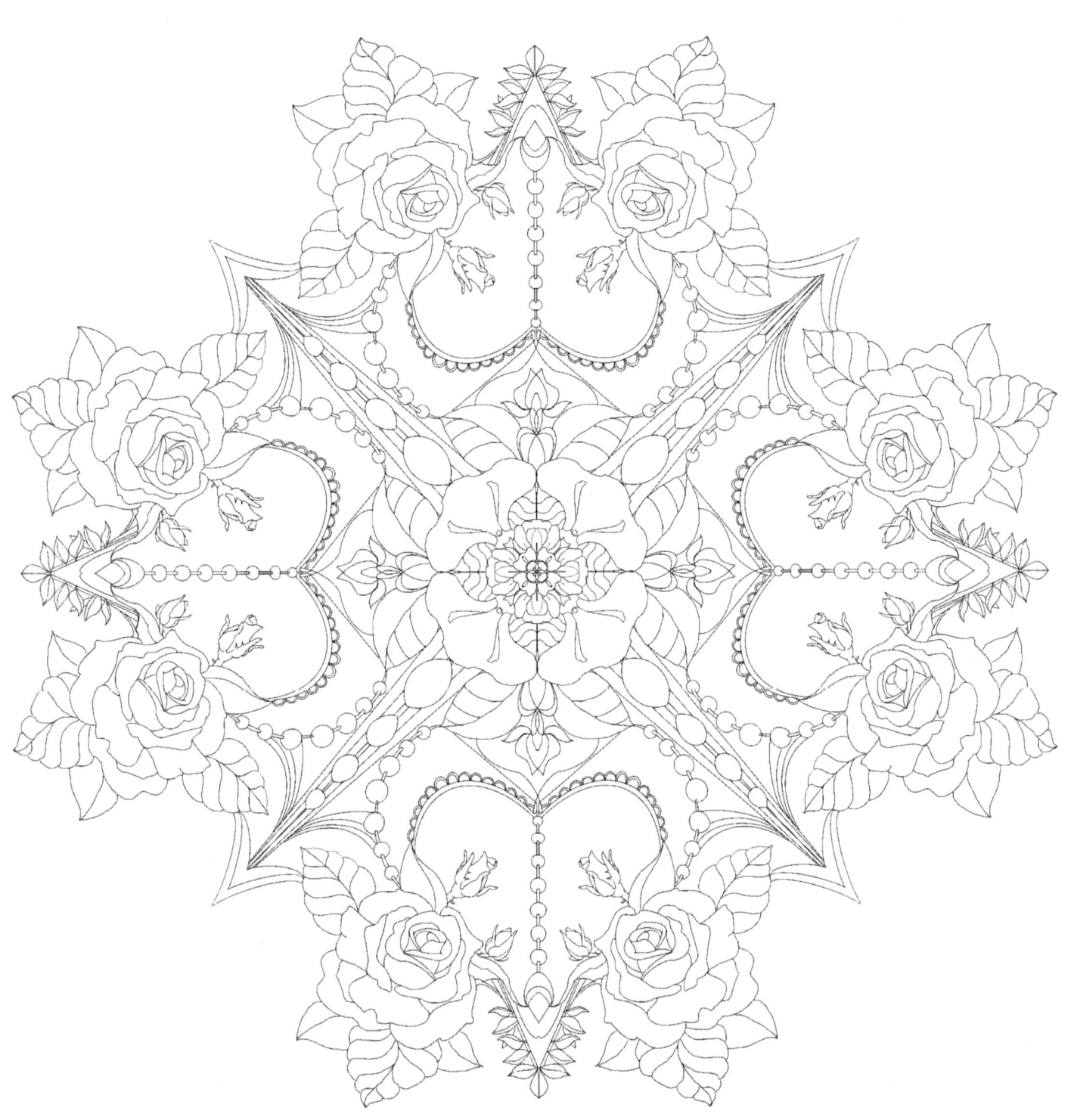

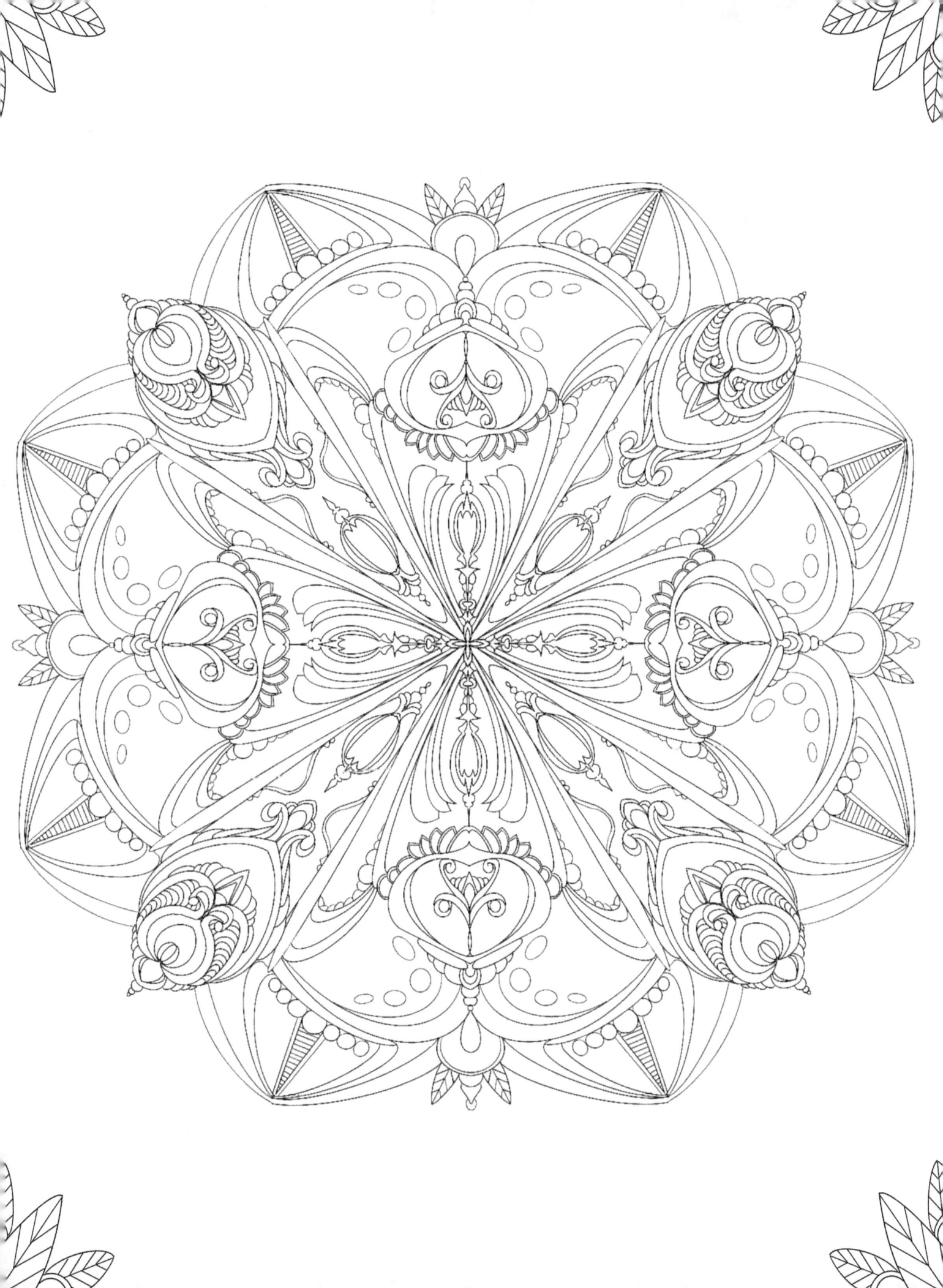

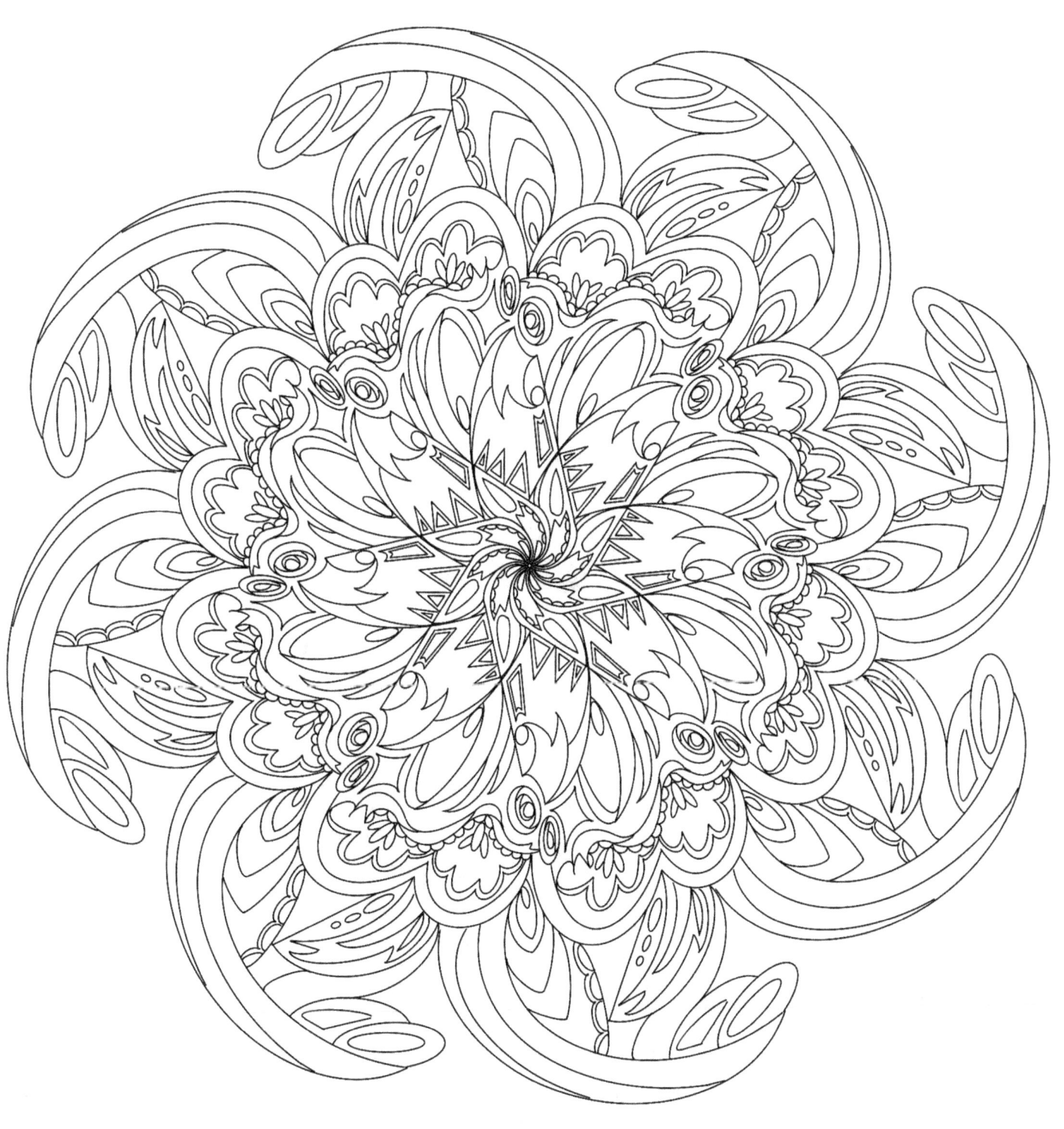

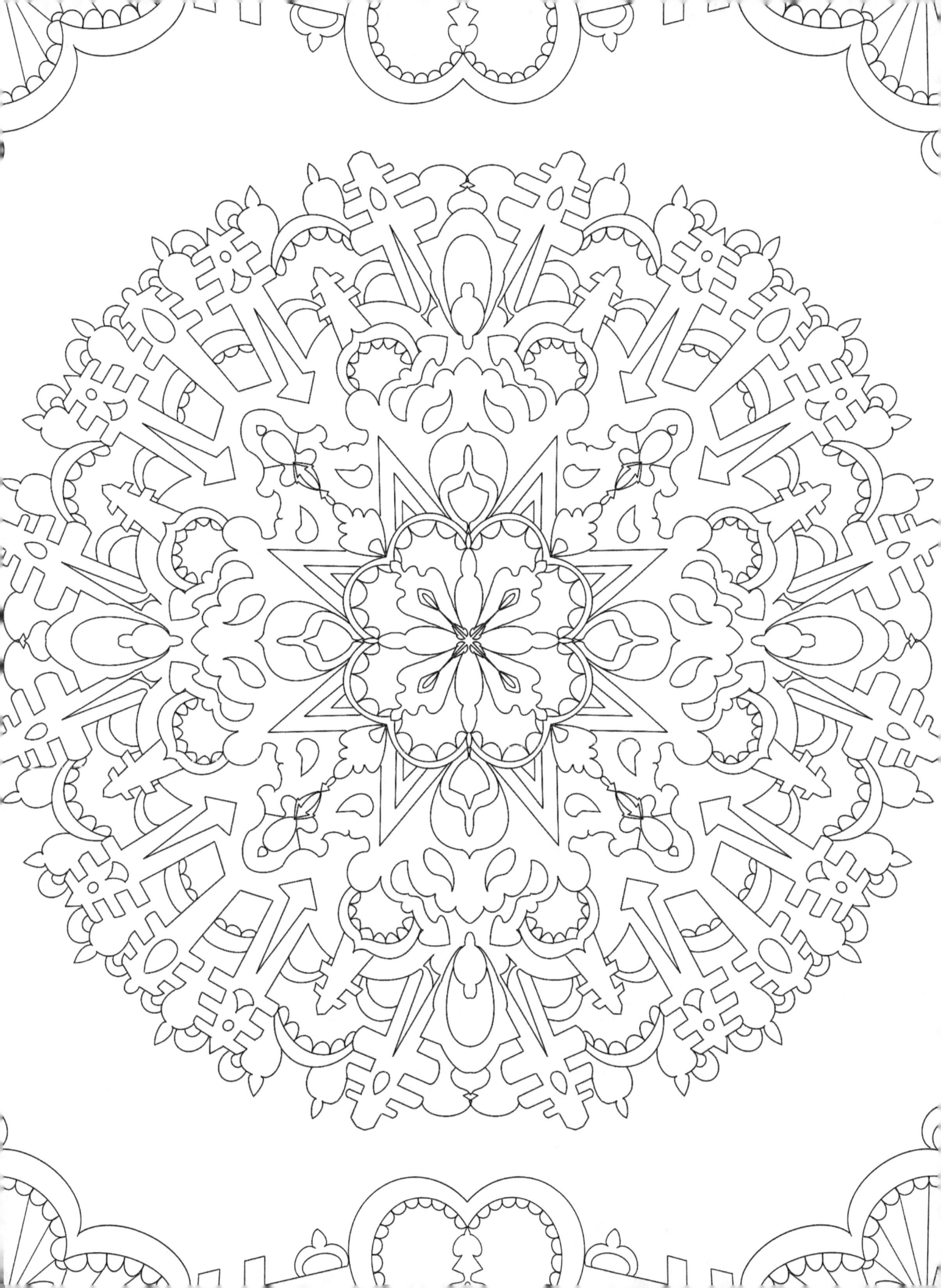

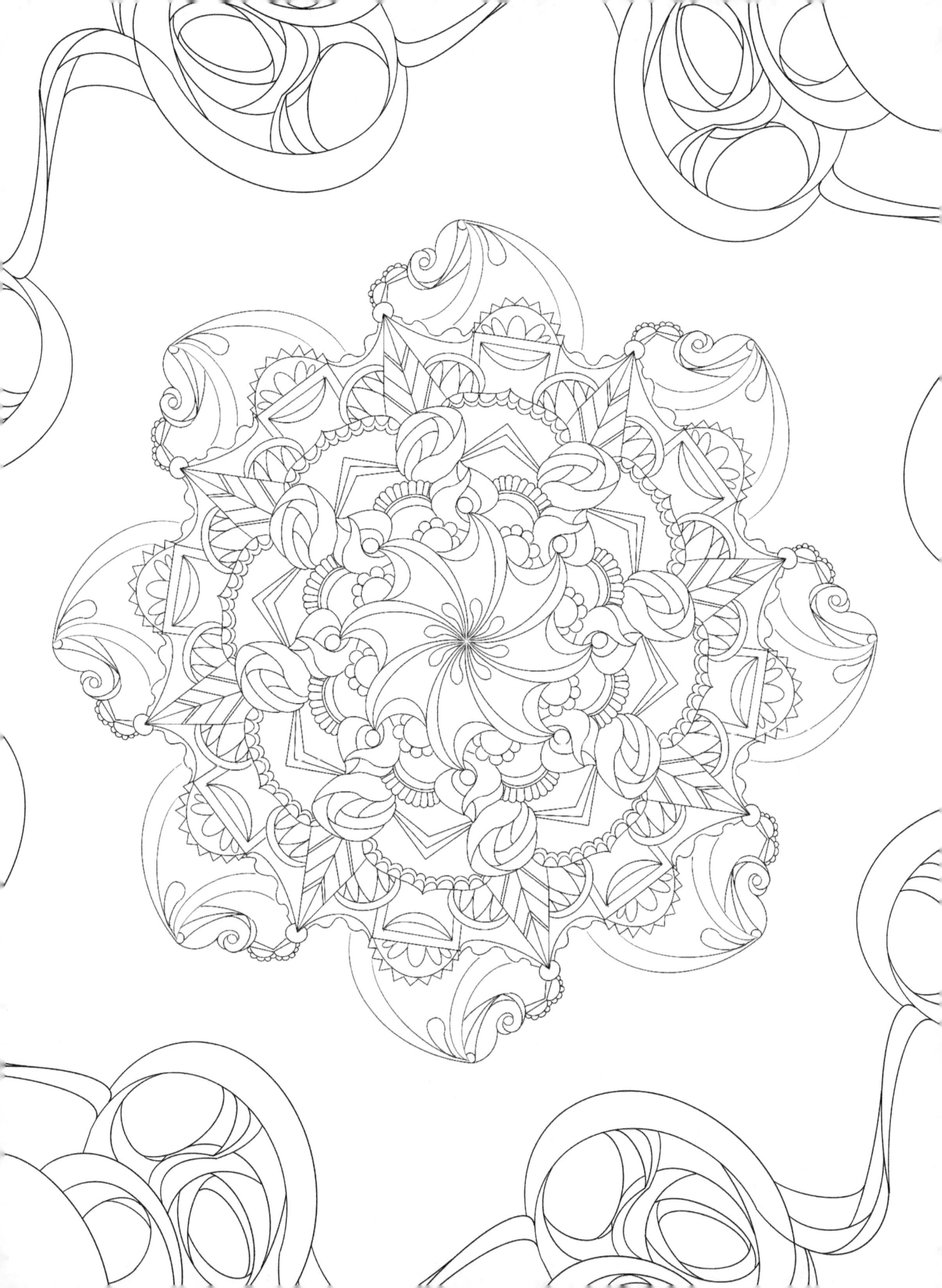

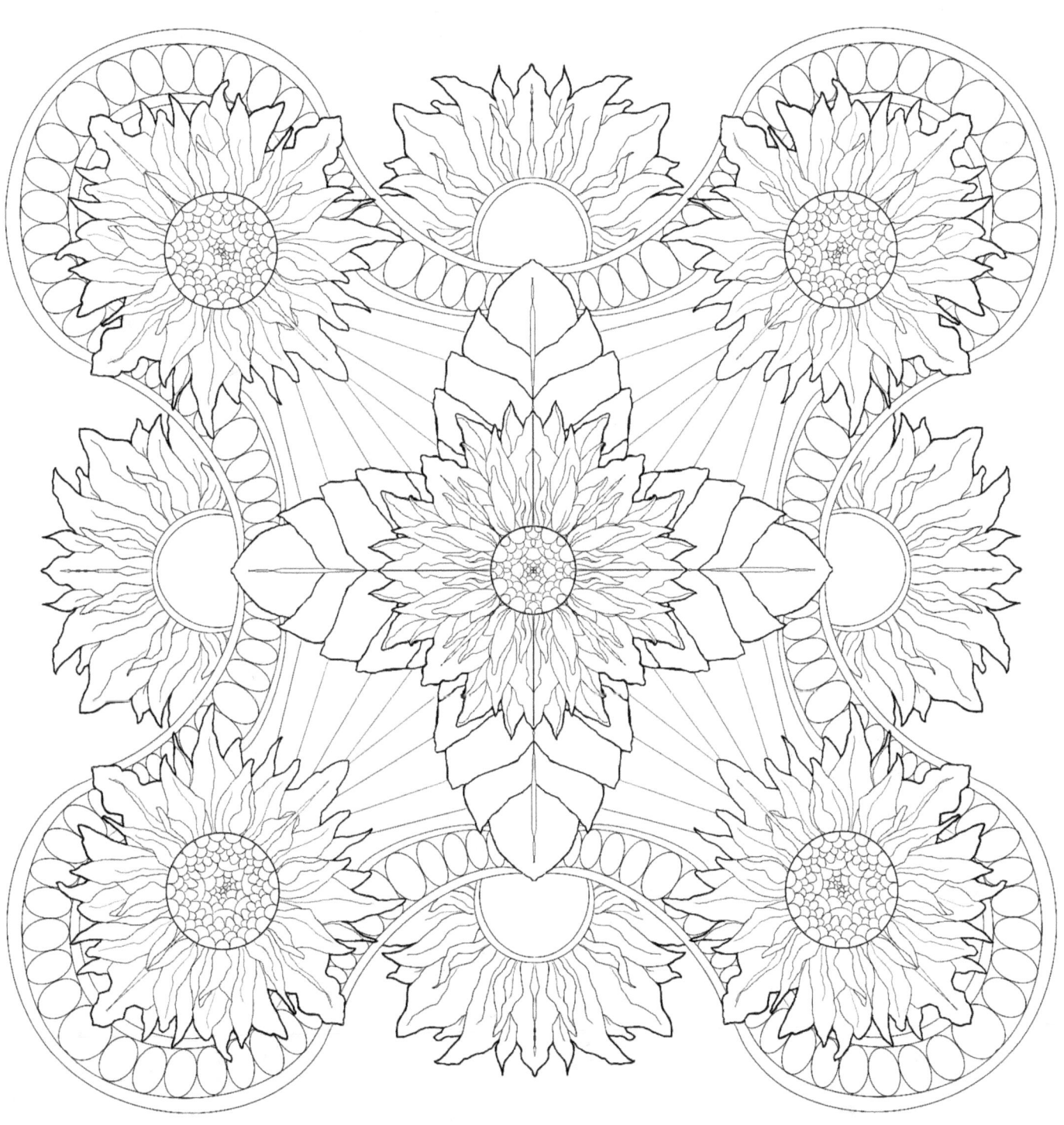

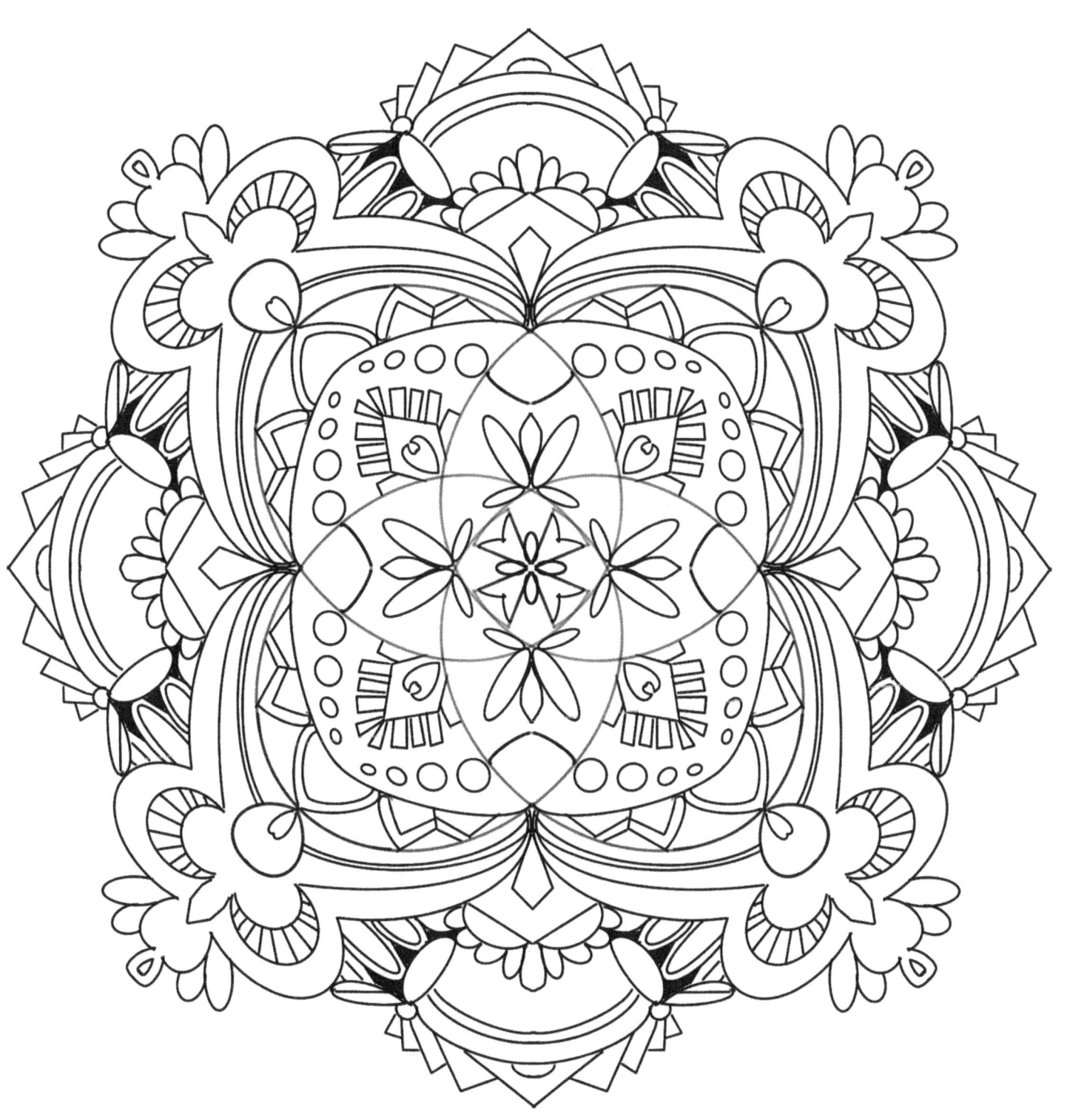

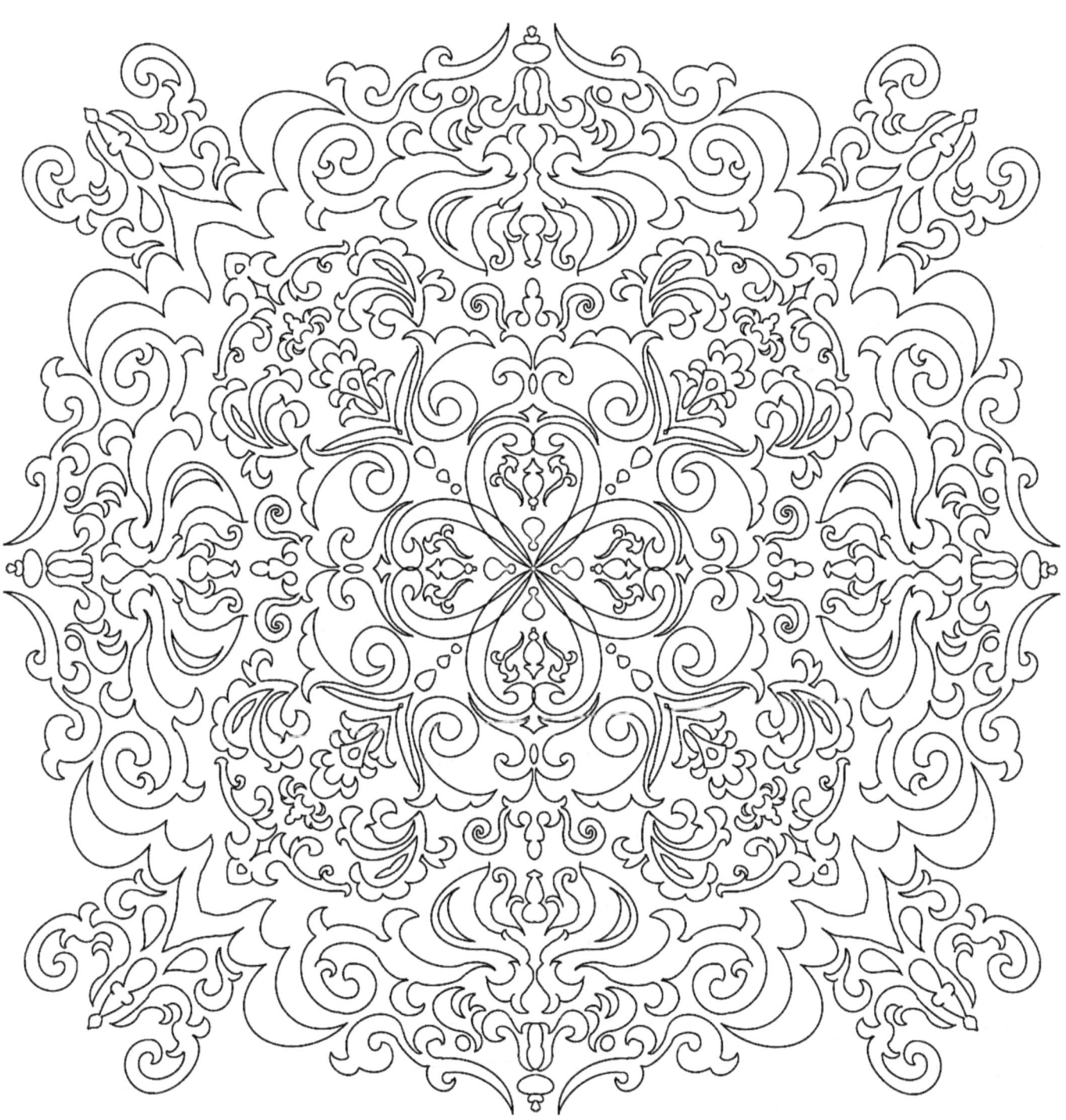

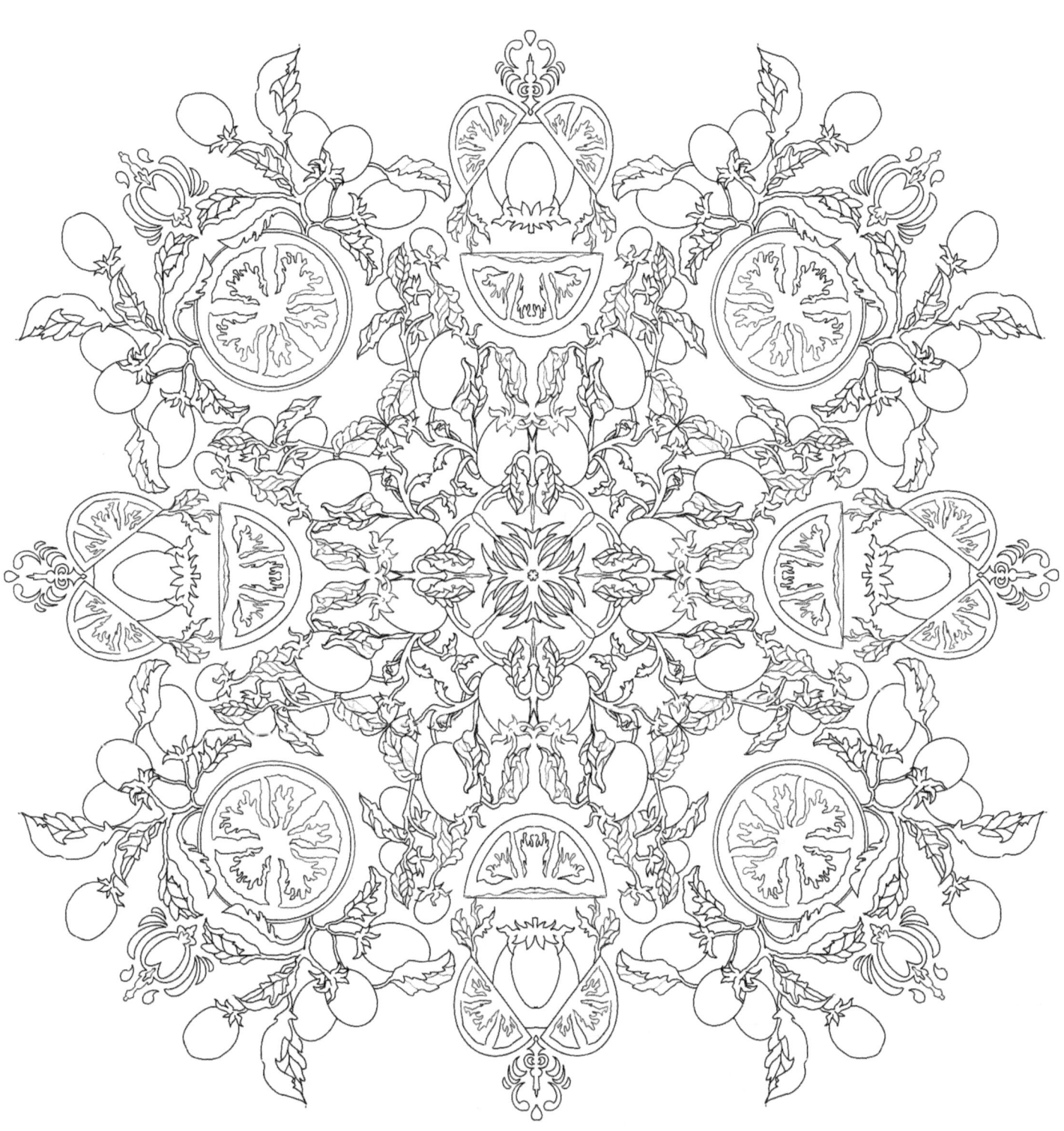

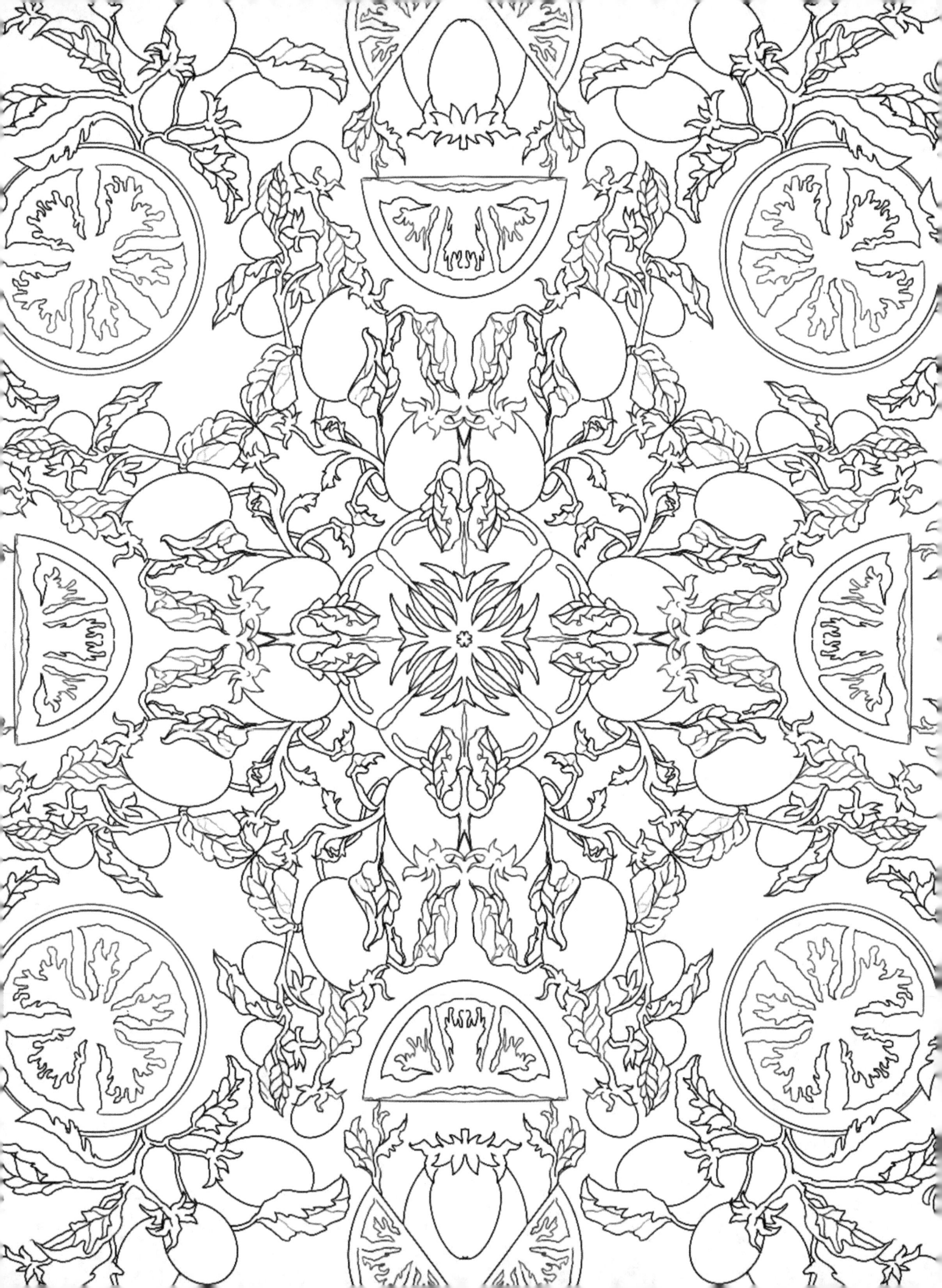

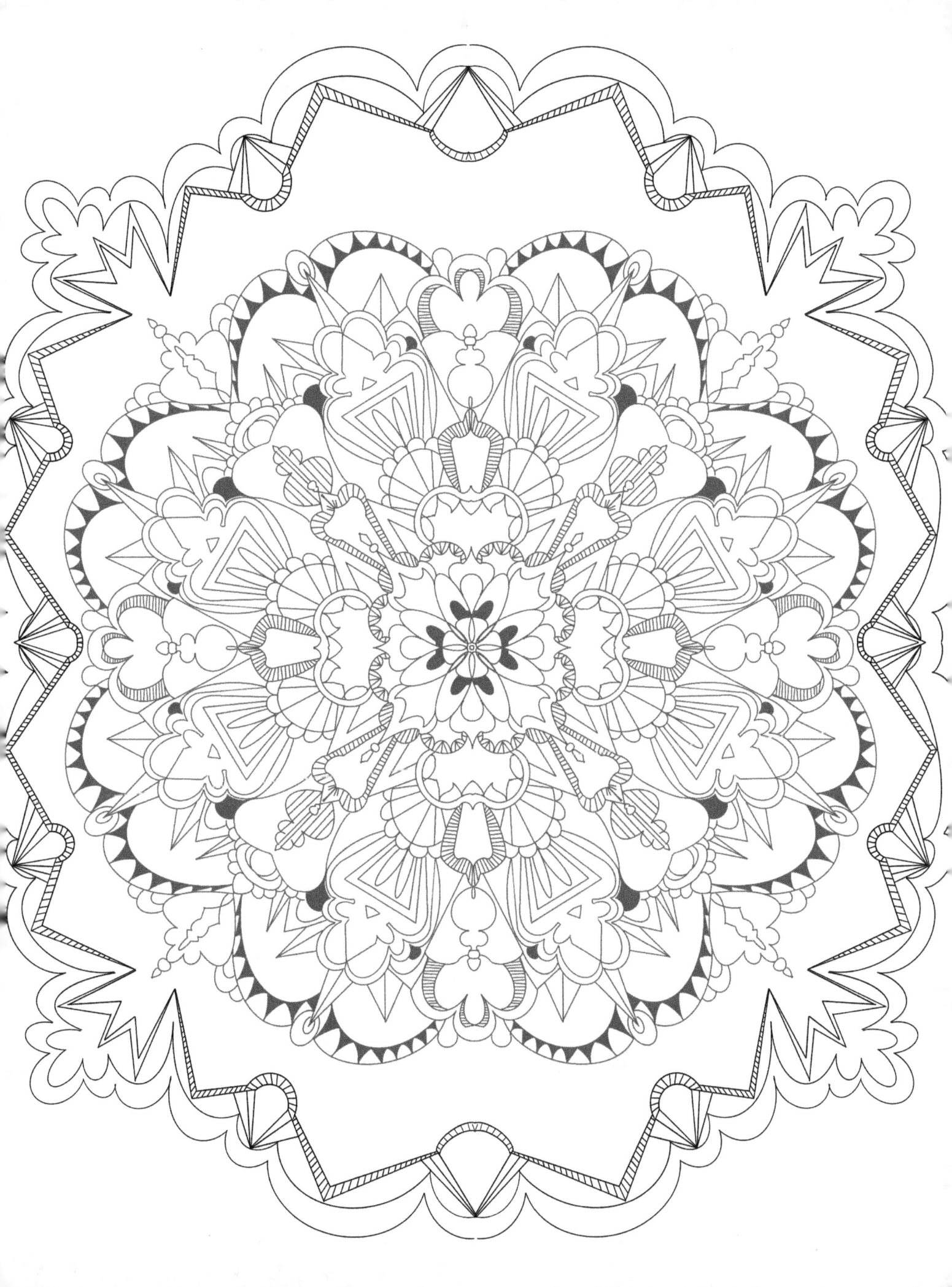

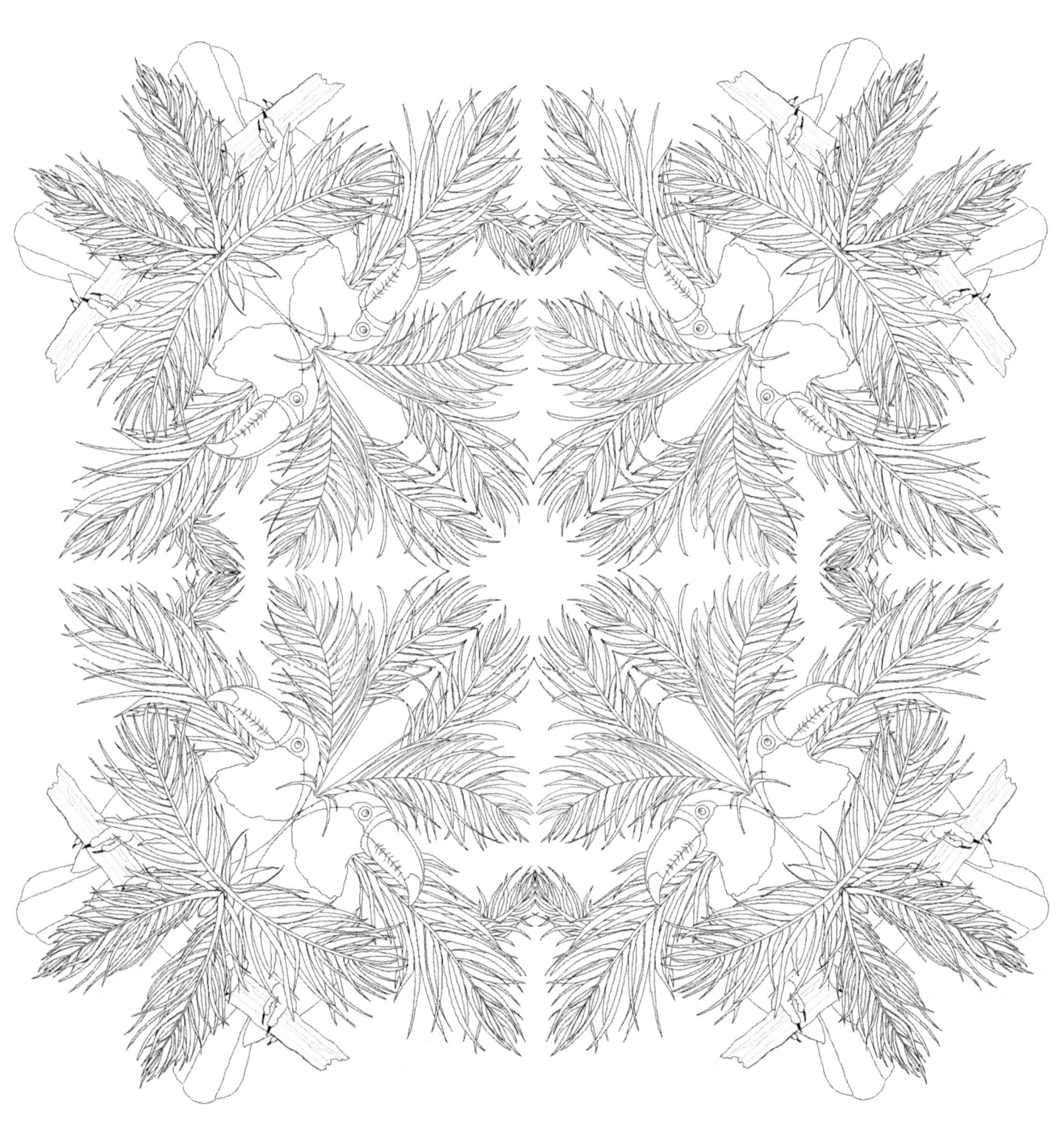

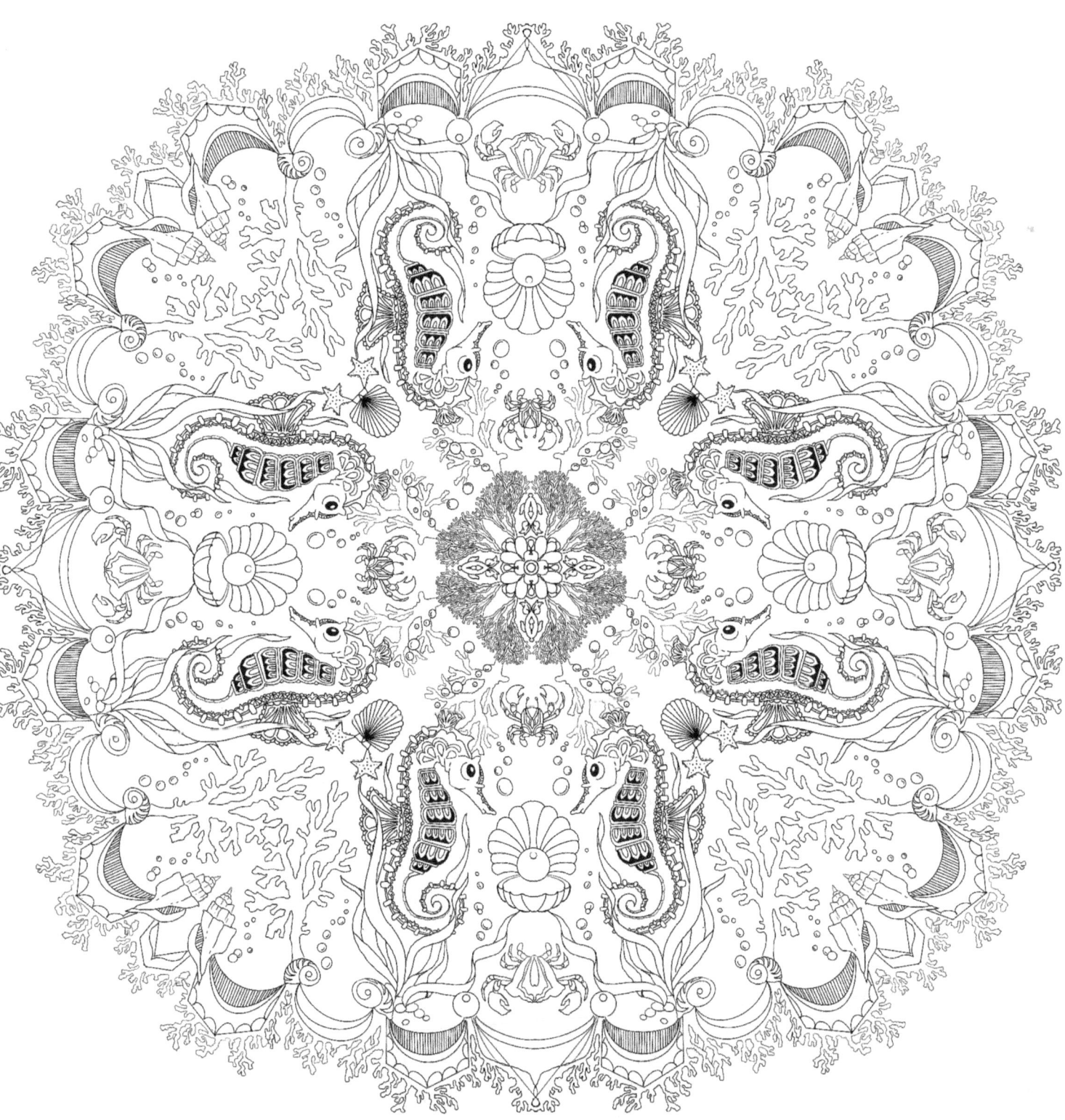

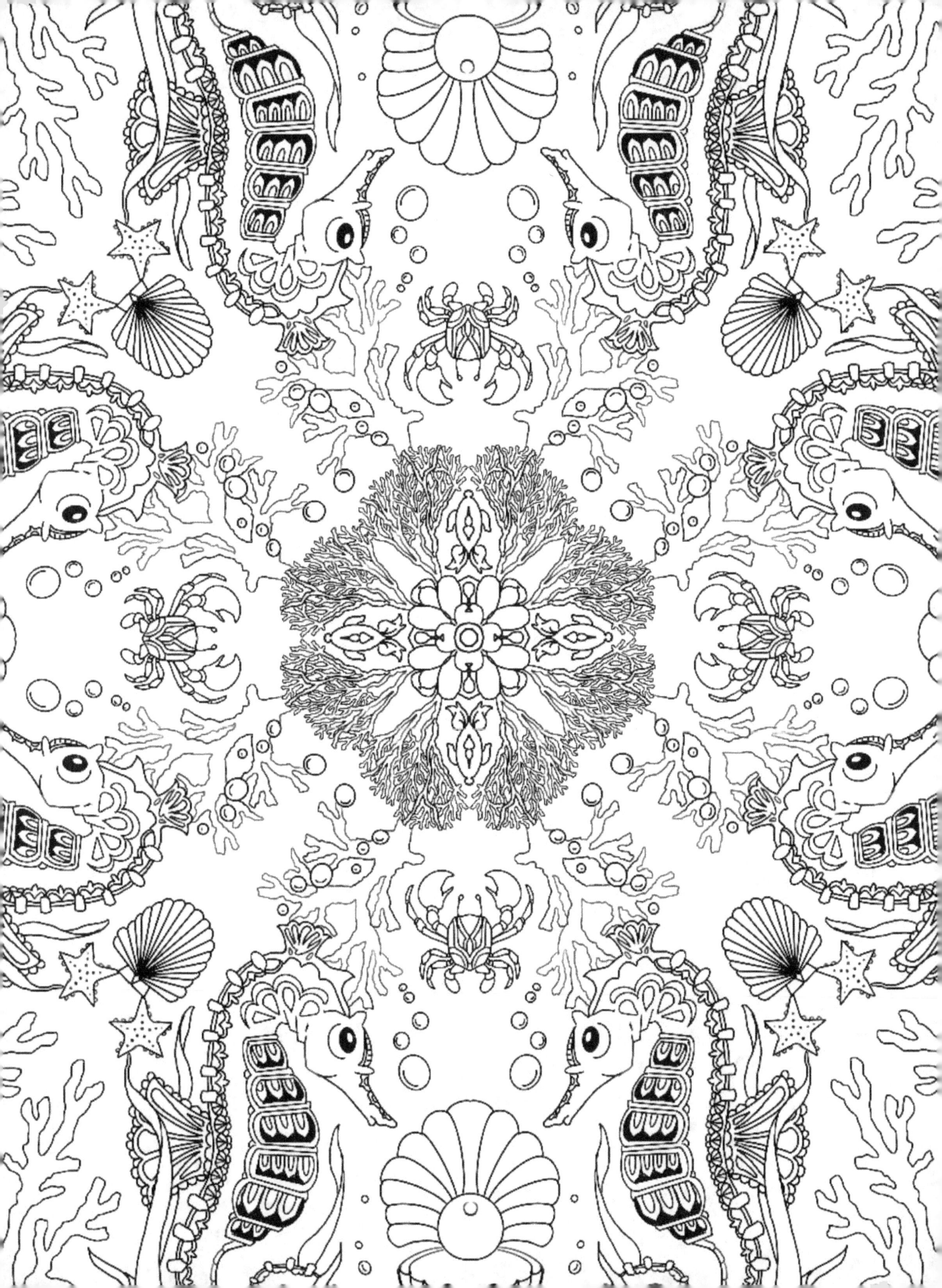

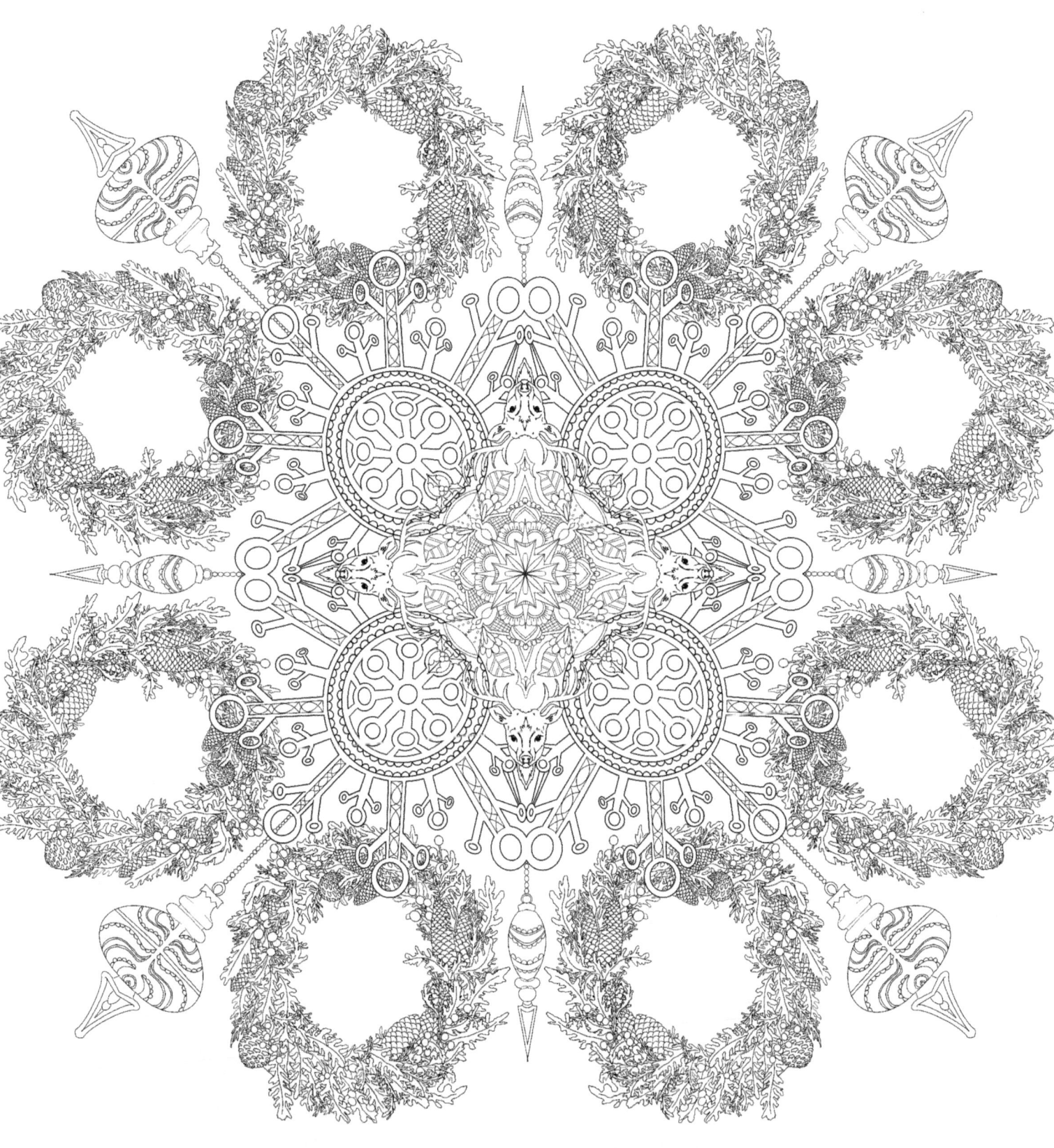

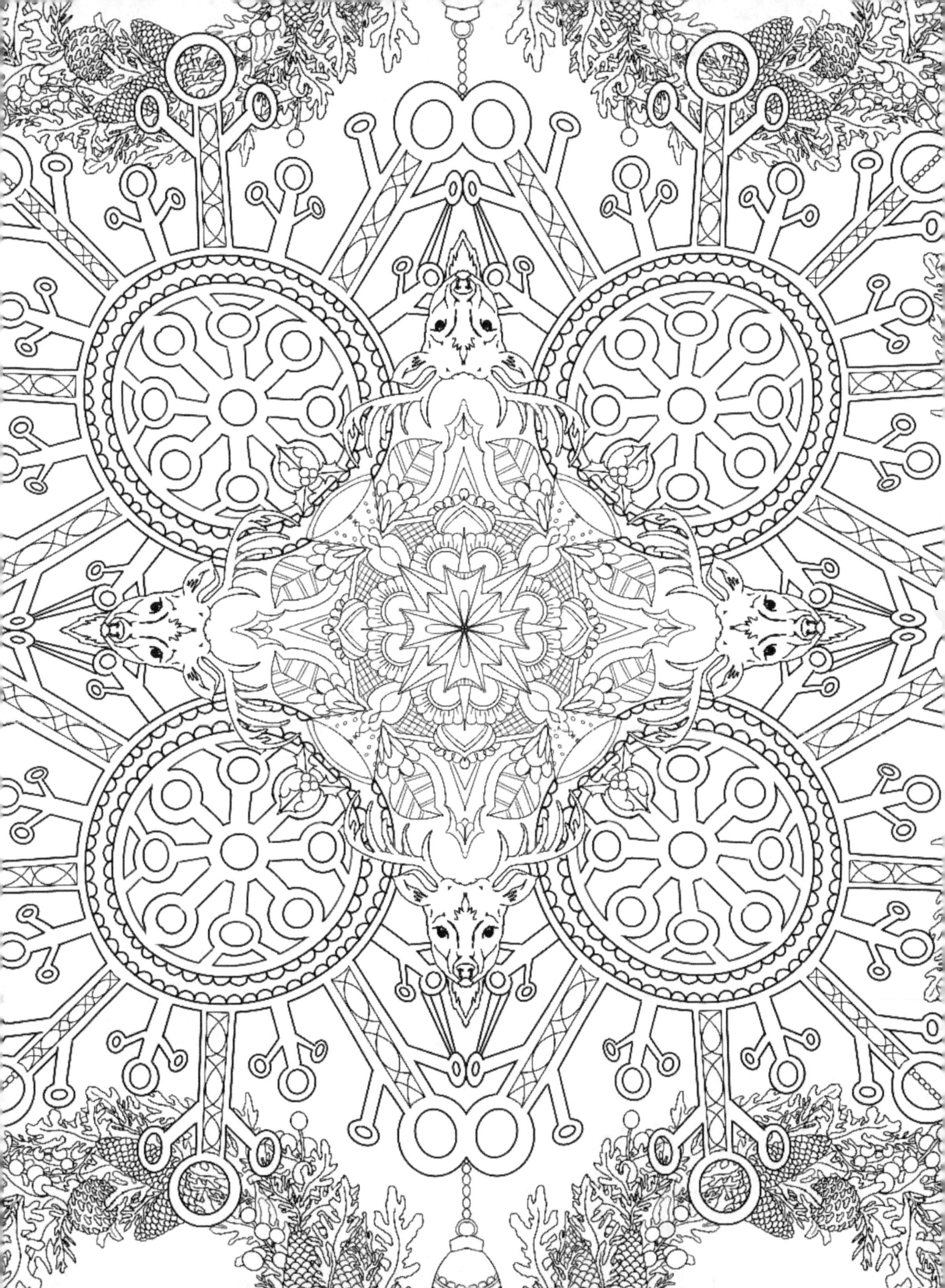

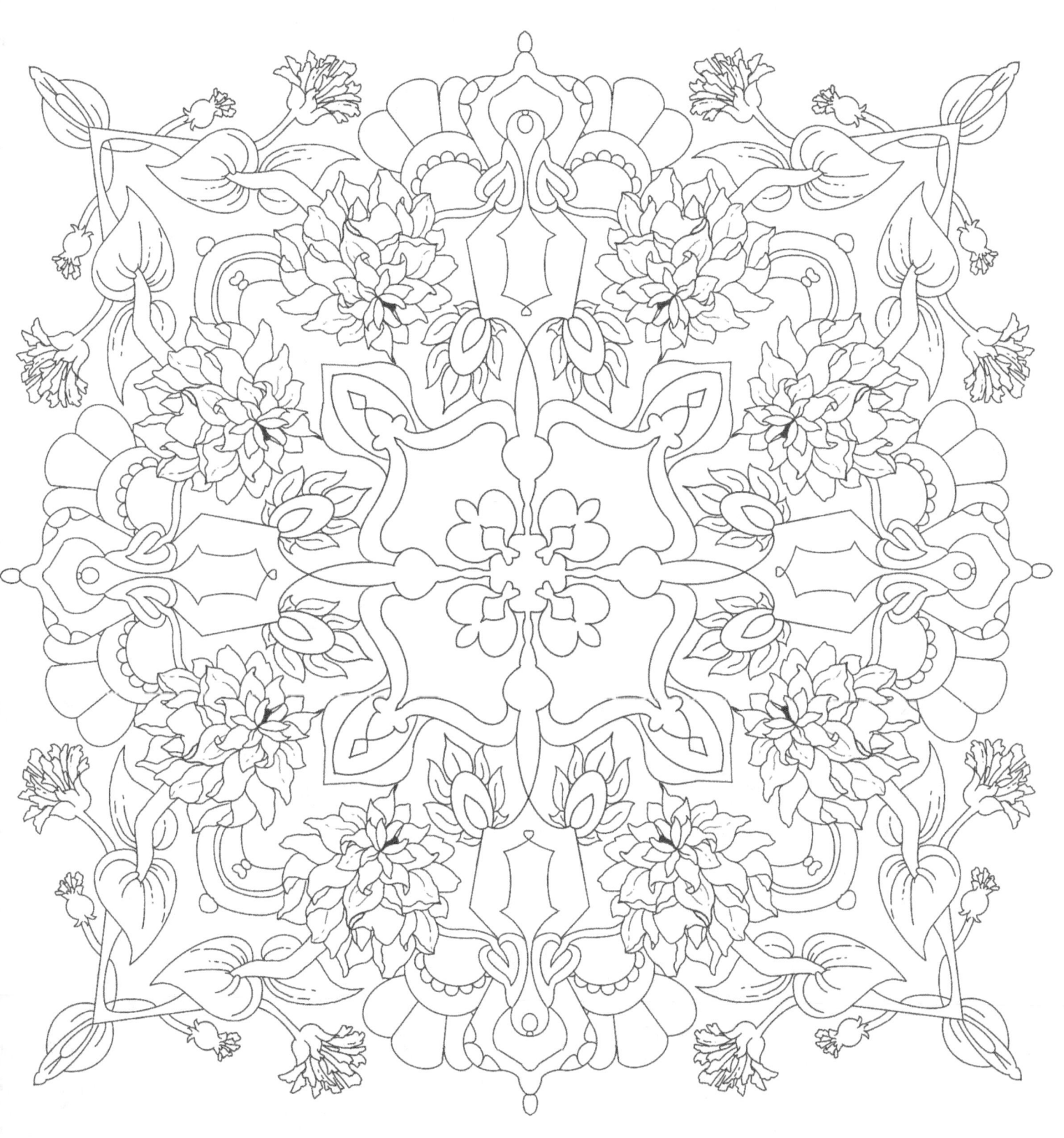

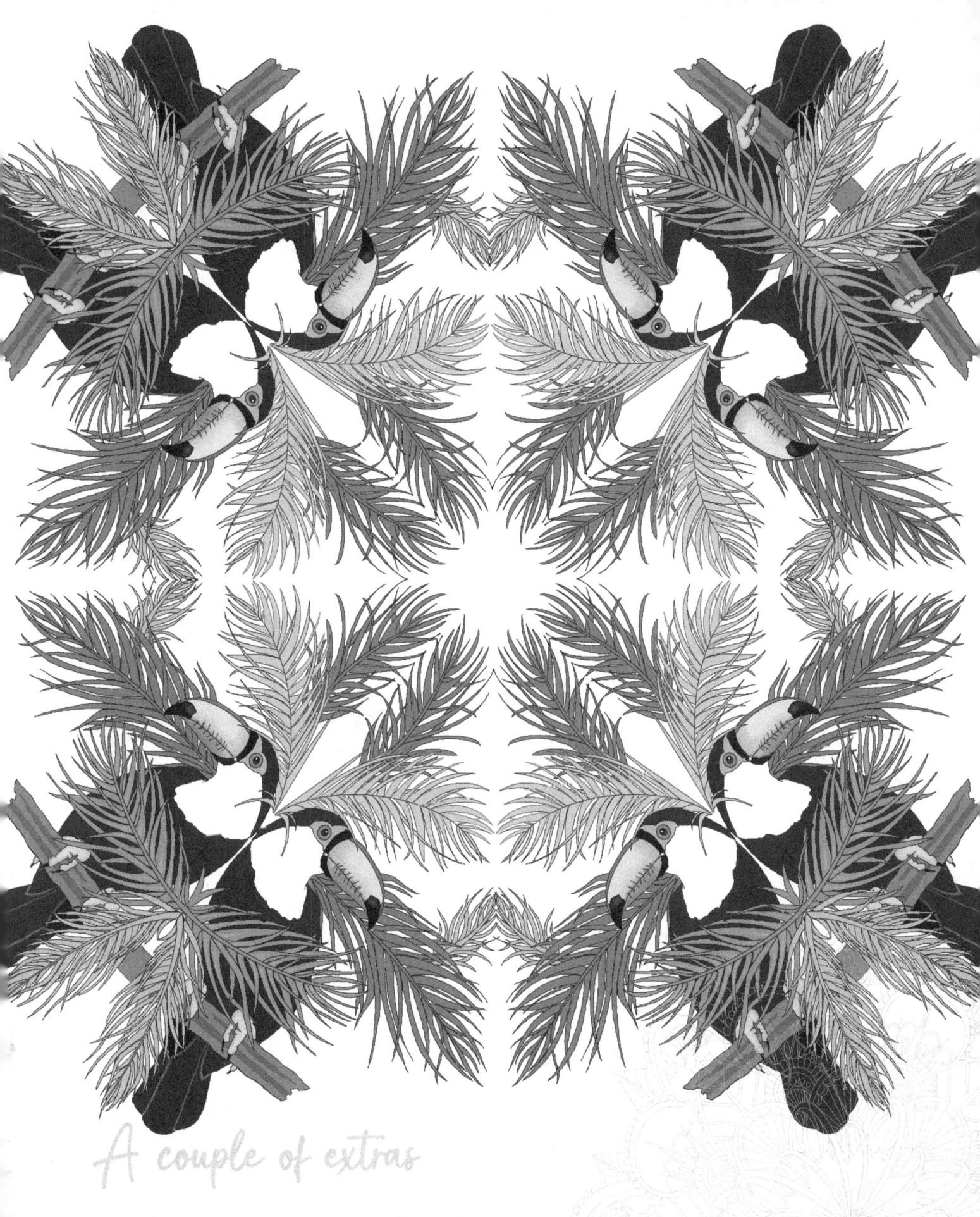

A couple of extras

For the young, or young at heart!

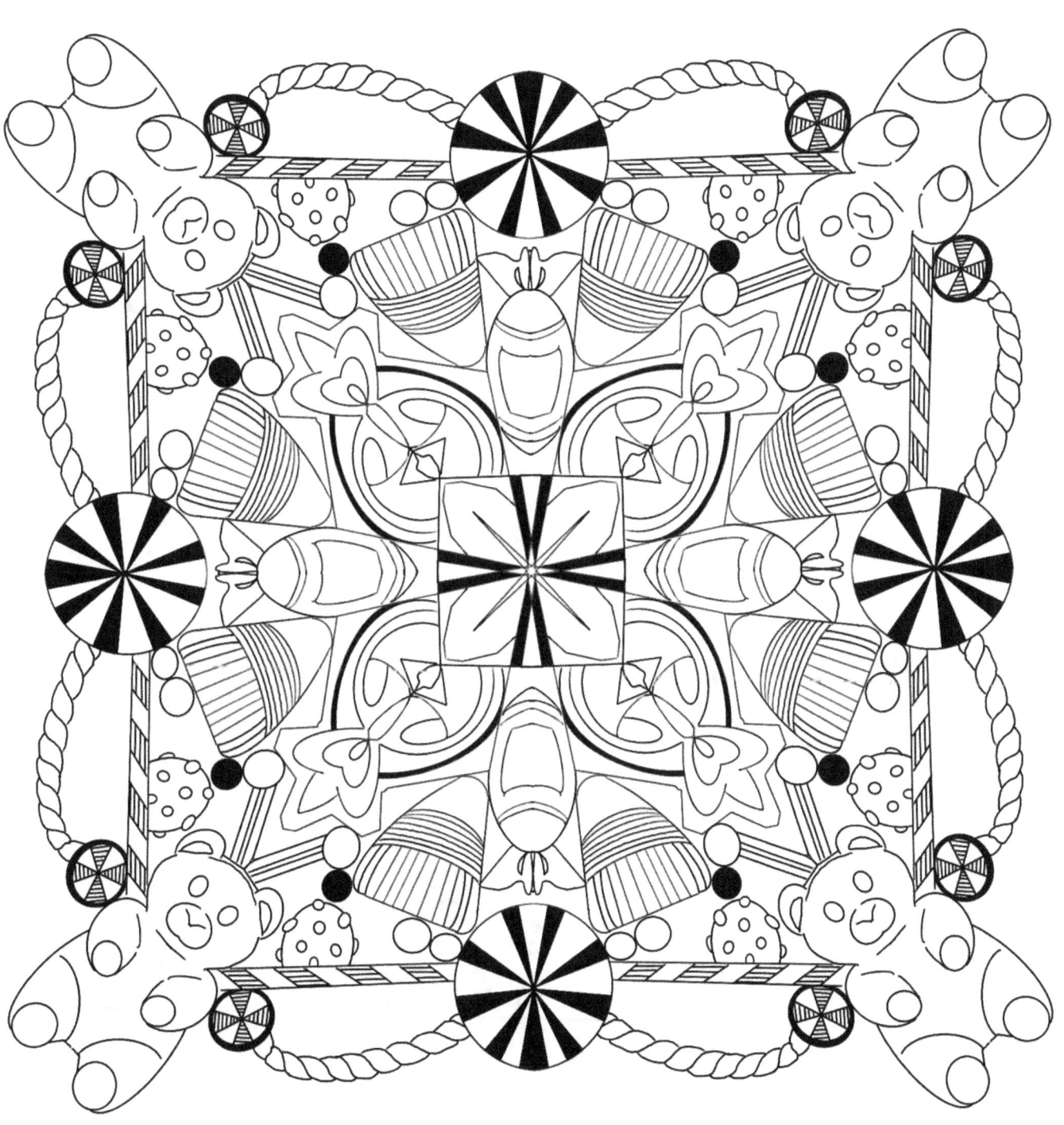

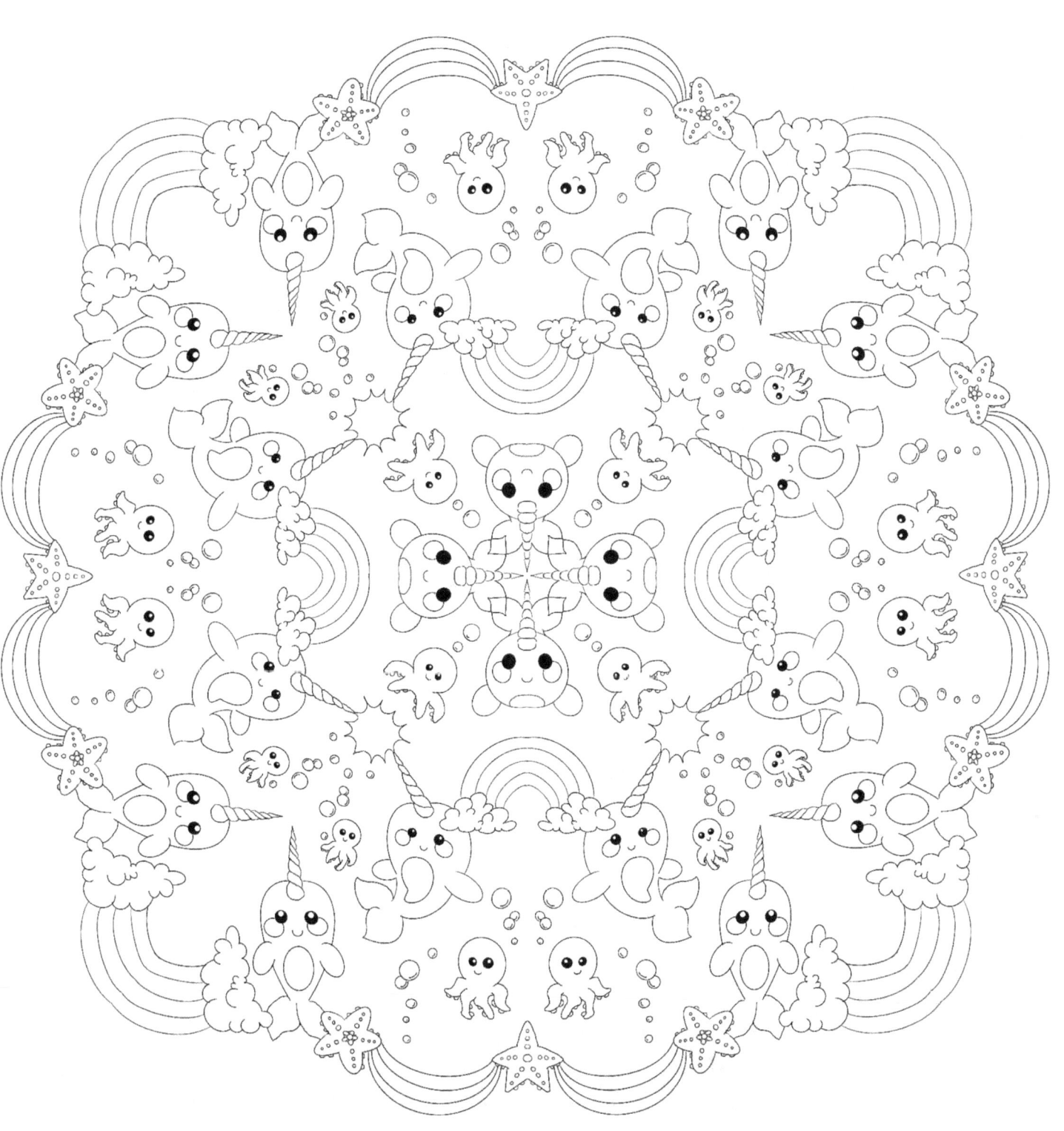